Kj's Food Journal
EVERYDAY
FAMILY RECIPES

DEDICATION

This book is dedicated to my loving family. My parents, my brother and sister, grandparents, aunties and uncles and my cousins, who have not only given me love and support but have also been the best guineapigs for all of these recipes. Without them, this book would be nothing.

EAT, *drink,* LAUGH, *and be happy!*

CONTENTS

INTRODUCTION **8**

BREAKFAST **10**

STARTERS, SNACKS & APPETISERS **44**

SIDES **76**

MAIN MEALS **100**

DESSERTS **158**

INDEX **201**

MEASUREMENT

LIQUIDS

Metric	Cup	Imperial
30ML		1 FL OZ
60ML	1/4 CUP	2 FL OZ
80ML	1/3 CUP	2 3/4 FL OZ
100ML		3 1/2 FL OZ
125ML	1/2 CUP	4 FL OZ
150ML		5 FL OZ
180ML	3/4 CUP	6 FL OZ
200ML		7 FL OZ
250ML	1 CUP	8 3/4 FL OZ
310ML	1 1/4 CUP	10 1/2 FL OZ
375ML	1 1/2 CUP	13 FL OZ
430ML	1 3/4 CUP	15 FL OZ
475ML		16 FL OZ
500ML	2 CUP	17 FL OZ
625ML	2 1/2 CUP	21 1/2 FL OZ
750ML	3 CUP	26 FL OZ
1L	4 CUP	35 FL OZ

OVEN TEMPERATURE

Celsius	Fahrenheit
120°	250°
150°	300°
160°	325°
180°	350°
190°	375°
200°	400°
230°	450°

CONVERSION

Australia / USA

Australia	USA
PLAIN FLOUR	ALL-PURPOSE FLOUR
ICING SUGAR	POWDERED SUGAR
WHITE SUGAR	GRANULATED SUGAR
CASTER SUGAR	SUPER-FINE SUGAR
CORNFLOUR	CORNSTARCH
CAPSICUM	BELL PEPPER
ZUCCHINI	COURGETTE
ROCKET	ARUGULA
THICKENED CREAM	HEAVY CREAM

Country / One Cup

Country	One Cup
AUSTRALIA	250G
NEW ZEALAND	250G
USA	240G
UK	225G

This book uses the Australian Metric System for all of the recipes.

 Gluten Free
 Dairy Free
 Nut Free
 Egg Free
 Vegetarian
 Vegan

INTRODUCTION

Everyday Family Recipes is my very first cookbook, and in a lot of ways, one of my most precious creations. This book is focused on helping the everyday family put delicious and easy recipes on their tables, no matter the occasion. All of the recipes are easy to make with simple, everyday ingredients - you're not going to find any truffle oil or black garlic in this book!

My goal is to help everyone enjoy their food and the simple act of preparing it for the people they love, because I think that anyone can cook with the right recipes and lots of love.

I really hope you enjoy this book as much as I enjoyed creating it for you, and I would like to thank every single person that has purchased a copy! So eat, drink, laugh and be happy!

Keeley Spencer x

CHAPTER 01
Breakfast

11 Basic Pancakes

A basic pancake recipe, perfect for your Sunday breakfast or brunch! Light and fluffy, these pancakes are super easy and quick to make with basic ingredients!

 **PREPTIME:** 5 MIN

 COOKTIME: 10-15 MIN

 **MAKES:** 9 PANCAKES

INGREDIENTS

1 1/2 cups self-raising flour
2 tbsp caster sugar
1 tsp baking powder
pinch of salt
250ml milk
2 eggs
100g margarine, melted

METHOD

1. Sift dry ingredients into a large bowl, mix together and make a well in the centre.
2. Pour wet ingredients into well and whisk thoroughly until well combined.
3. For each pancake, scoop around 1/4 cup of batter onto a large, lightly oiled frying pan on medium heat. Cook until bubbles start to form, around 2-3 mins and flip. Cook for a further 2-3 mins.

Breakfast Board

Anyone that knows me knows that I absolutely love nibble platters. From cheese boards to graze boards and even fruit trays, I love being able to pick and munch on a variety of goodies spread out in front of me. So why not bring that concept to the breakfast table?!

 PREPTIME: 10 MIN

 COOKTIME: 30 MIN

 SERVES: 2-3 PEOPLE

INGREDIENTS

1 tbsp oil
4 rashers bacon (see note)
3 beef sausages
2 eggs
6 cherry tomatoes
1/2 cup baby spinach

NOTES

It's 100% optional to thread the bacon onto skewers. I just like the way it looks on the platter!

METHOD

1. Add oil to a large frying pan on medium heat. Cook sausages and bacon to your liking and remove from pan.
2. Add eggs and cherry tomatoes to the pan, season with salt and pepper and cook eggs to your liking. Remove from pan along with cherry tomatoes.
3. Slice sausages in half and carefully thread bacon onto skewers, being careful as it will be hot. Place on serving board.
4. Carefully add eggs to board and fill the gaps with spinach. Place cherry tomatoes on top of spinach and serve.

15 Stuffed Breakfast Tomatoes Four Ways

To prepare tomatoes for stuffing, slice in half and using a spoon, scoop out the tomato pulp and seeds. Stuff with one (or more) of the following fillings!

Spinach & Mushroom

Finely dice 4 small button mushrooms and add to a bowl along with 1/2 cup ricotta cheese and 1/4 cup chopped baby spinach. Mix to combine and divide between 4 halves of prepared tomatoes. Top each one with 1 tbsp grated cheese and cook at 180°C in either an air fryer for 10-12 mins or 15-20 mins in an oven.

Cheese & Bacon

Whisk together 2 eggs and salt & pepper, to taste. Add 1/4 cup grated cheese, 1 rasher diced shortcut bacon, 2 finely diced garlic cloves, 1/4 tsp cayenne pepper and 2 tbsp chopped fresh chives and stir until well combined. Divide egg mixture between 4 halves of prepared tomatoes, being careful not to overfill them. Cook at 180°C in either an air fryer for 10-12 mins or 15-20 mins in oven.

Baked Egg

Season four large prepared tomato halves with salt, to taste. Crack 1 egg into each tomato and season with salt & pepper. Top each egg with 1/2 tsp diced fresh chives and 1/8 tsp cayenne pepper. Cook at 180°C in either an air fryer for 8-10 mins or 12-15 mins in oven or until eggs are cooked to your liking.

Vegetable Medley

Whisk together 2 eggs and salt & pepper, to taste. Add 1/4 cup grated cheese, 1/4 cup diced capsicum, 1/4 cup grated zucchini, 2 finely diced garlic cloves, 1 paprika and 1/2 tsp garlic salt and stir until well combined. Divide egg mixture between 4 halves of prepared tomatoes, being careful not to overfill them. Cook at 180°C in either an air fryer for 10-12 mins or 15-20 mins in oven.

19 Savoury Mince & Egg

Savoury Mince on Toast is a classic Australian dish that's hard not to love. This version is topped with a fried egg for a delicious and hearty breakfast that is sure to be a hit!

 PREPTIME: 5 MIN

 COOKTIME: 20 MIN

 SERVES: 4 PEOPLE

INGREDIENTS

FOR THE MINCE
1 tbsp oil
1/2 onion, diced
1 carrot, diced
1 clove garlic, finely diced
500g beef mince
2 tbsp worcestershire sauce
1 tbsp gravy powder
1/4 cup tomato sauce
300ml beef stock
salt & pepper, to taste
1/4 cup peas

TO SERVE
1 tbsp oil
4 eggs
4 slices toast

METHOD

1. Heat oil in a large frying pan and sauté onion and carrot until tender. Add garlic and mince. Cook, stirring with a wooden spoon to break up mince, for 6 to 8 minutes or until browned. Add worcestershire sauce, gravy powder, tomato sauce, stock and peas and stir to combine. Allow to simmer until reduced, about 10-15 mins. Remove from heat.
2. Meanwhile, in a separate frying pan, add oil and fry eggs to your liking. Remove from pan and season with salt and pepper. Set aside.
3. Divide mince between four plates and top each with a fried egg. Serve with toast.

21 Brekky Wraps

These easy brekky wraps are the perfect thing to wake up to any day of the week! Loaded with all the good stuff, this is a delicious way to start your day!

 PREPTIME: 5 MIN

 COOKTIME: 25 MIN

 SERVES: 4 PEOPLE

 NF

INGREDIENTS

FOR THE WRAPS
1 tbsp oil
4 middle rashers bacon
4 eggs
salt & pepper, to taste
1 avocado
4 soft wraps
1 tomato, sliced

FOR THE RELISH
1 tbsp butter
2 red onions, sliced
1 tbsp brown sugar
1 tbsp red wine vinegar

NOTES
The onion relish can be made ahead of time and stored in a jar in the fridge until needed.

METHOD

1. Heat oil in a large frying pan on medium heat and add bacon. Cook until slightly crispy or cooked to your liking. Remove from pan and place on a plate with paper towel.
2. Add eggs to pan and fry to your liking. Remove from pan and season with salt and pepper. Set aside.
3. Meanwhile, for the relish, melt butter in a saucepan on medium heat and add onions. Sauté until just tender and add sugar and red wine vinegar.
4. Stir and allow to simmer for 20 minutes, stirring regularly to prevent sugar from burning. Once reduced and a dark red colour, remove from pan. You can store any leftover relish in a jar in the fridge for later use.
5. To assemble the wraps, mash up avocado in a small bowl and season with salt and pepper. Divide between wraps and add tomatoes, bacon and egg. Top with onion relish and serve.

23 Smashed Avo with Feta

Smashed Avo (or smashed avocado for the non Australians) has got to be Australia's national breakfast dish. And as an Aussie dedicated to boosting the awareness for Australian Cuisine, I'm sharing a great little recipe to help you start the day like a champion.

 PREPTIME: 5 MIN

 COOKTIME: 2 MIN

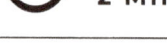 **SERVES:** 4 PEOPLE

INGREDIENTS

2 avocados
4 tbsp lemon juice
salt & pepper, to taste
8 slices of turkish bread (see notes)
50g feta cheese

METHOD

1. Add avocado and lemon juice to a small bowl and roughly mash with a fork until at desired consistency. Season to taste with salt and pepper. Set aside.
2. Toast or grill turkish bread until golden and spread mashed avocado onto each slice.
3. Crumble feta cheese over top and serve.

NOTES
If you can't find turkish bread, you can substitute for sour dough or any other kind of bread you prefer.

"try serving this dish with a poached egg"

25 Bacon & Egg Toast Cups

Bacon & egg toast cups are a quick and easy breakfast cooked in 20 minutes. Baked in individual ramekins – or cook them in a muffin tin – this is my new favourite way to eat bacon & eggs on toast! A super simple breakfast idea and definitely kid friendly!

PREPTIME: 5 MIN

COOKTIME: 10-15 MIN

SERVES: 4 PEOPLE

INGREDIENTS

4 slices of bread
4 rashers of shortcut bacon
4 eggs
salt & pepper, to taste
1/8 tsp cayenne pepper (optional)
2 tbsp chives, finely diced
1/4 cup grated cheese

NOTES

If you would like to make more than four at a time, or don't have ramekins, this recipe can also be made in a muffin tin.

METHOD

1. Preheat oven to 180°C.
2. Line four small ramekins with a slice of bread. Add a rasher of bacon to the ramekins, leaving enough of a well for the egg to sit in.
3. Crack an egg in each ramekin and season to taste with salt & pepper, a dash of cayenne pepper, chives and grated cheese.
4. Cook in oven for 10-15 mins.
5. Run a knife around the edge of each ramekin to loosen and remove.

27 Easy Shakshuka

Shakshuka is a Middle Eastern and North African dish that is usually served for breakfast. It's a simple and nutritious dish made from simmering tomatoes along with onion, garlic, spices and poached eggs. For me, it's an extremely comforting dish that warms the soul and tastes amazing.

 PREPTIME: 5 MIN

 COOKTIME: 40 MIN

 SERVES: 4 PEOPLE

   (V) (NF) (DF)

INGREDIENTS

1 tbsp olive oil
1/2 onion, diced
2 garlic cloves, finely diced
1/3 red capsicum, diced
2 x 500g cans of crushed tomatoes
1/2 tsp paprika
1/8 tsp cayenne pepper
1/2 tsp garlic salt
3 sprigs fresh thyme leaves
1/2 tbsp fresh parsley
salt & pepper, to taste
4 eggs
4 slices toasted turkish bread

NOTES
This recipe is gluten-free if you serve with gluten-free bread or no bread at all!

METHOD

1. Dice onion and capsicum and add to a large frying pan on medium heat, along with garlic and oil.
2. Cook until golden and add tomatoes, paprika, cayenne pepper, garlic salt and season to taste with salt and pepper. Stir to combine. Add herbs, stir and allow to simmer for two mins.
3. Make four small wells in the tomato sauce and crack an egg in each one. Cover frying pan with a lid and let steam for 20-25 mins or until eggs are cooked to your liking. Garnish with fresh parsley and serve with toasted turkish bread.

28

Shakshuka is a delicious dish of eggs poached in a spiced tomato sauce! Yum!

31 French Toast with Bacon & Maple Syrup

If you're looking for an easy and delicious breakfast, you really can't go past French Toast...it's a classic for a reason! Made within minutes, it really is perfect for any day of the week!

 PREPTIME: 2 MIN

 COOKTIME: 15 MIN

 SERVES: 4 PEOPLE

INGREDIENTS
2 tsp butter
4 eggs
50ml milk
salt & pepper, to taste
8 slices of bread

TO SERVE
4 rashers of bacon
maple syrup

NOTES
You don't have to serve French Toast with bacon! Try fresh fruit, Nutella & banana, ice cream or just simple icing sugar!

METHOD
1. Heat 1 tsp of butter in a frying pan on medium heat until melted.
2. Crack eggs into a shallow bowl and beat with milk until well combined. Season with salt and pepper.
3. Dip a slice of bread in egg, turning to coat both sides evenly.
4. Cook in frying pan until golden brown on both sides and remove from pan. Repeat with remaining slices, adding more butter as necessary.
5. Meanwhile, pan fry bacon until cooked to your liking and serve with french toast and maple syrup.

Sausage & Potato Breakfast Hash

If you've never heard of it, then you need to know all about the delicious meal known as the Hash. A 'hash' is a great little dish of chopped-up meats, potatoes, and onions that are fried up all together in a pan.

PREPTIME: 5-10 MIN

COOKTIME: 30-35 MIN

SERVES: 2 PEOPLE

INGREDIENTS

2 medium-sized potatoes
1/2 red onion
1/3 green capsicum
1 clove garlic
2 beef sausages
1 tbsp oil
salt & pepper, to taste
1 tsp smoked paprika
2 tbsp worcestershire sauce
200ml beef stock

METHOD

1. Peel, wash and dice potatoes, onion, capsicum and sausages into 3/4-inch pieces. Finely dice the garlic.
2. Heat oil in a large frying pan over medium heat. Add prepared ingredients to pan and fry off, stirring occasionally until the meat has browned and the onions have softened.
3. Add paprika, worcestershire sauce and season to taste with salt and pepper. Stir to combine and allow to cook for 1-2 mins. Add beef stock and turn the heat to high. Allow to simmer until all the liquid has reduced and the vegetables begin to fry and crisp up.
4. Once the potatoes are tender, remove from heat and serve.

Cheesy Spinach Omelette

Starting the day with a healthy portion of cheese is always a good thing! If you agree, then this cheesy spinach omelette is the perfect breakfast for any day of the week!

 PREPTIME: 5-10 MIN

 COOKTIME: 5 MIN

 SERVES: 1 PERSON

INGREDIENTS

2 large eggs
1 clove garlic, finely diced
salt & pepper, to taste
1 tbsp butter
1/4 onion, finely diced
1/4 cup baby spinach
15g feta cheese
1/4 cup grated cheese

METHOD

1. In a small bowl, whisk together eggs, garlic, salt and pepper until thoroughly combined.
2. Melt butter in a large frying pan on medium heat and add egg mixture. Scatter over onion, spinach, crumbled feta and grated cheese.
3. Allow to cook for 1-2 mins and, using an egg flip, fold the egg in half on itself. Allow to cook for another 1-2 mins and remove from pan. Serve.

37 Creamy French Baked Eggs

This creamy egg dish is an easy and quick breakfast recipe that you can make in under 30 minutes! Creamy eggs baked in ramekins are the perfect breakfast or brunch that will be the highlight of your morning!

 PREPTIME: 5 MIN

 COOKTIME: 15-20 MIN

 SERVES: 4 PEOPLE

INGREDIENTS

2 slices leg ham, roughly chopped
3/4 cup thickened cream
4 eggs
salt & pepper, to taste
1/8 tsp cayenne pepper
1/4 cup cheese, grated
fresh parsley, to serve (optional)
4 sliced toasted baguette

NOTES

This recipe can easily be made gluten-free by using gluten-free bread or omitting bread altogether!

METHOD

1. Preheat oven to 200°C.
2. Divide ham between four ramekins and add cream, reserving 4 tbsp for later use.
3. Crack an egg into each ramekin and season with salt, pepper and cayenne. Add 1 tbsp of cream to each and sprinkle with grated cheese.
4. Bake for 15-20 mins or until eggs are cooked to your liking. Serve with parsley and toasted baguette.

THERE'S NOTHING MORE DISAPPOINTING THAN AN EGG NOT COOKED TO YOUR LIKING.

CHAPTER 02

Starters, Snacks & Appetisers

45 Potato, Leek & Bacon Soup

Sometimes it really is hard to believe that such simple ingredients could make something so good...but sometimes less really is more when it comes to a delicious meal, and this recipe proves it!

 PREPTIME: 5-10 MIN

 COOKTIME: 1 HOUR 10 MIN

 SERVES: 4 PEOPLE

INGREDIENTS

1 tbsp oil
2 cloves garlic, finely diced
2 rashers shortcut bacon, diced
2 large leeks, sliced
2 large potatoes, peeled & chopped
1L chicken stock
2 sprigs fresh thyme
500ml milk
salt & pepper, to taste
cream, to serve
1 extra rasher of bacon, to serve

METHOD

1. Add oil to a large saucepan on medium heat. Add garlic, bacon and leeks and sauté until leeks are tender.
2. Add potatoes, stock and thyme and bring to a gentle simmer. Cover and cook for 15-20 mins or until potato is tender and fully cooked, stirring occasionally.
3. Remove thyme sprigs and take off the heat. Blitz until smooth with a stick blender. Return to heat, stir through milk and season with salt and pepper.
4. Meanwhile, fry remaining rasher of bacon until crispy and dice into small pieces.
5. Serve soup with a dollop of cream and bacon bits.

Quick & Easy Spaghetti Marinara

If anyone knows me, they'll know that I adore pasta! This recipe is one of my go to's for when a craving strikes and the tomatoes are at their best!

 PREPTIME: 5 MIN

COOKTIME: 55 MIN

SERVES: 4 PEOPLE

INGREDIENTS

8 large roma tomatoes
2 tbsp olive oil
salt & pepper, to taste
2 cloves garlic, finely diced
1 tsp fresh oregano, roughly torn
1 tsp fresh chives, diced (optional)
1/4 tsp ground nutmeg
1 tsp sugar
300g dried spaghetti
parmesan cheese, to serve
fresh parsley, to serve (optional)

METHOD

1. Preheat oven to 180°C and cut tomatoes in half. Place them skin side up on a baking tray and drizzle with 1 tbsp olive oil. Season with salt and pepper and roast for 45 mins. Allow to cool and remove skins.
2. Add remaining oil to a medium sized saucepan on medium heat and gently sauté garlic until golden. Add tomatoes and break up using a wooden spoon. Stir to combine.
3. Add herbs, nutmeg and sugar and bring to a gentle simmer. Season to taste with salt and pepper.
4. Allow to cook for a few mins to reduce slightly, around 5-10 mins and remove from heat.
5. Meanwhile, place a large pot of water on high heat, bring to the boil and add a generous amount of salt. Add spaghetti and cook according to packet instructions. Drain the pasta in a colander and set aside.
6. Add spaghetti to the saucepan and toss through the sauce to cover. Divide into serving bowls and serve with parmesan and parsley.

This is one of my favourite meals to make...it's heap, easy and uses basic ingredients. What more could you want?

Pico de Gallo Nachos

Nachos are my definite go-to snack for times when I'm stuck for inspiration. I always seem to have just enough ingredients to whip up some variation, like this basic vegetarian one!

 PREPTIME: 10 MIN

 COOKTIME: 15 MIN

 SERVES: 4 PEOPLE

INGREDIENTS

FOR THE CHIPS
8 garlic tortillas
4 tbsp olive oil
1 tbsp paprika
salt & pepper, to taste

TO SERVE
1 cup cheddar cheese, grated
2 tomatoes
1 lime, juiced
salt & pepper, to taste
4 tbsp sour cream
fresh basil, for garnish

METHOD

1. Preheat oven to 180°C. Oil and season tortillas with salt, pepper and paprika and cut each one into 8 triangles. Cook in oven for 5-8 mins or until golden, making sure to keep a close eye on them.
2. Lightly sprinkle over grated cheese and cook for another 2-5 mins or until melted. Remove from oven straight away to avoid burning.
3. Meanwhile, dice tomato and add to small bowl along with lime juice and season to taste with salt and pepper. Stir to combine.
4. Once tortilla chips have cooled slightly, place them on a serving plate and top with tomato salsa and sour cream. Garnish with basil if desired and serve.

51 Classic Cob Loaf

A classic cob loaf is an adored party favourite that just about everyone seems to love. This cob loaf recipe is my easy and quick go-to recipe for any occasion! Your guests will be sure to love it!

 PREPTIME: 5 MIN

 COOKTIME: 20-25 MIN

 SERVES: 8 PEOPLE

INGREDIENTS

1 cob loaf
1 onion, diced
2 cloves garlic, finely diced
2 spring onions, thinly sliced
100g bacon, diced
250g cream cheese, softened
150ml cream
2/3 cup sour cream
1 1/2 cups grated cheese
pepper, to taste

METHOD

1. Preheat oven to 180°C and line a large baking tray with baking paper. Set aside.
2. Cut 4cm off the top of cob loaf. Scoop out the centre of loaf, leaving 1.5cm edge and tear into pieces.
3. For the filling, add remaining ingredients to a microwave safe bowl and stir thoroughly to combine. Microwave in 30 second increments for 2 mins, stirring in between, or until cheese just starts to melt.
4. Spoon mixture into loaf and place on prepared baking tray. Arrange lid and bread pieces around loaf in a single layer. Bake for 20 mins or until golden brown. Serve immediately.

53 Beetroot, Red Onion & Feta Tarte Tatin

This Beetroot, Red Onion and Feta Tarte Tatin is a fresh and easy appetiser or light meal! The sweet, earthy flavours of the beetroot pair so well with the caramelised onion and salty feta cheese! This Tarte Tatin is sure to impress!

 PREPTIME: 10 MIN

 COOKTIME: 50-55 MIN

 MAKES: 6-8 SLICES

INGREDIENTS

1 x 165g sheet puff pastry
1 tbsp oil
2 tbsp butter
2 garlic cloves, finely diced
1 red onion, sliced
500g beetroot, peeled, cut into wedges
1 tbsp balsamic vinegar
1 tbsp brown sugar
salt & pepper, to taste
1 egg, beaten
25g feta cheese
1/4 cup fresh rocket

METHOD

1. Preheat oven to 180°C and set pastry aside to defrost if using frozen. Gently heat oil and butter in a large frying pan over medium heat until butter has melted.
2. Add garlic and onion and cook until onions are slightly tender. Add beetroot to frying pan and stir until everything is evenly coated in butter.
3. Add balsamic vinegar, sugar and season to taste with salt and pepper. Cook for 15 mins, stirring occasionally.
4. Spoon beetroot and onions into a 20cm pie dish, making sure the beetroots are cut side up. Bake in the oven for 15 mins.
5. Remove from oven and cover with pastry, tucking the edges into the sides of the pie dish to fit tightly around the filling. Brush with beaten egg and bake for 20-25 mins or until pastry is golden brown.
6. Leave to stand for 10 mins before inverting onto a serving plate. Sprinkle with crumbled feta and rocket leaves. Serve.

Tomato Bruschetta
55

If anyone knows me well, they'll know that I LOVE tomatoes. Meaning, I would probably eat them every day in many different forms. And one of the best ways to use tomatoes, in my opinion, is Bruschetta!

 PREPTIME: 5 MIN

 COOKTIME: 5 MIN

 SERVES: 4 PEOPLE

INGREDIENTS

1 tbsp olive oil
8 slices crusty sourdough bread
2 cloves garlic
4 ripe tomatoes, diced
1/4 red onion, diced
1 tbsp fresh basil, finely sliced
1 lime, juiced
2 tsp balsamic vinegar
salt & pepper, to taste

METHOD

1. Brush olive oil on both slides of each slice of bread. Gently toast bread in a frying pan on medium heat until slightly golden on each side. Slice garlic cloves in half and rub down both sides of each slice of toasted bread. Set aside.
2. Add tomato, onion, basil, lime juice and balsamic vinegar to a bowl and mix until thoroughly combined. Season to taste with salt and pepper and divide tomato mixture onto each slice of bread, reserving the liquids. Serve immediately.

57 Beetroot & Pistachio Dip

This Beetroot & Pistachio Dip recipe is an easy and simple recipe for entertaining! Made with fresh beetroot, feta & cream cheese and finished off with crushed pistachio nuts, this is a real crowd pleaser!

 **PREPTIME:** 5 MIN

 **SERVES:** 6-8 PEOPLE

METHOD

1. Add cream cheese, feta, beetroot, garlic, lemon and oil to a food processor and blitz until smooth.
2. Season to taste with salt and spoon into serving bowl. Sprinkle with crumbled feta and pistachios.

INGREDIENTS

125g cream cheese
1/2 cup diced feta cheese, plus extra to serve
250g cooked, peeled beetroot
1 clove garlic
1/4 lemon, juiced
1 tbsp olive oil
salt, to taste
5 pistachios, shelled and crushed

NOTES

To make this dip nice and easy, I've used precooked beetroot but you can definitely roast your own at home!

59 Spinach & Feta Dip

I love the simple combination of spinach and feta! It's one of my favourite dip flavours and I knew that I had to make my own version at home! My spinach and feta dip is an easy and creamy party favourite!

 PREPTIME: 5 MIN

 **SERVES:** 6 PEOPLE

INGREDIENTS

125g cream cheese
1/2 cup diced feta, plus extra to serve
1/2 cup baby spinach
1 clove garlic
1/4 lemon, juiced
1 tbsp olive oil
salt, to taste

METHOD

1. Add cream cheese, feta, spinach, garlic, lemon and oil to a food processor and blitz until smooth.
2. Season to taste with salt and spoon into a serving bowl. Sprinkle with extra feta cheese. Serve.

NOTES

Try serving this dip with 'Cheats' Tortilla Chips! (p. 71)

Roasted Capsicum Bean Dip

Are you looking for a tasty appetiser recipe that's dairy and gluten free? Well this Roasted Capsicum Bean Dip is perfect for you! Made in less than five minutes, it's a great go to for easy entertaining!

PREPTIME: 5 MIN

SERVES: 6-8 PEOPLE

GF | DF | V | EF | NF | VG

INGREDIENTS

1 x 400g can cannellini beans, drained

1 cup sliced roasted peppers, drained (see notes)

1 clove garlic

1/4 lemon, juiced

1 tbsp olive oil

salt, to taste

1/4 tsp paprika

fresh parsley, for garnish (optional)

NOTES

I used jarred roasted peppers but you could easily roast your own capsicum if you prefer.

METHOD

1. Add the beans, roasted peppers, garlic, lemon juice, and oil to a food processor and blitz until smooth and creamy, adding more juice and oil if needed. Season to taste with salt.
2. Spoon into serving bowl and sprinkle with paprika. Garnish with parsley, if using. Serve with pita bread or tortilla chips.

Sticky Honey-Soy Chicken Wings

There's just something about chicken wings that makes them so addictive, so lovable. It's probably the thought of tearing into a chunk of juicy, delicious meat with your teeth and feeling the sticky sauce all over your face…..sorry, I think I just started drooling a little bit.

 PREPTIME: 5 MIN

 COOKTIME: 45-50 MIN

 SERVES: 4 PEOPLE

INGREDIENTS

12 chicken wings
1/3 cup honey
1/3 cup soy sauce
3 tbsp sesame seeds

NOTES

The longer these chicken wings marinate for, the tastier they will be!

METHOD

1. Add chicken wings to a large bowl along with honey and soy sauce. Marinate for 1-2 hours.
2. Preheat oven to 180°C. Place chicken wings in a baking dish and sprinkle sesame seeds over top.
3. Bake for 30 mins and turn wings over before basting with pan juices. Continue to cook for a further 15-20 mins or until wings are dark brown and cooked through.

67 Mediterranean Layered White Bean Dip

This dip is great served with just about anything from tortilla or pita chips to raw veggies such as carrot and celery sticks or any kind of crackers! I like to serve it spread out on a platter because it makes for prettier presentation and is easier to scoop up a good mix of toppings!

 PREPTIME: 5-10 MIN

 COOKTIME: 2 MIN

 SERVES: 6-8 PEOPLE

   GF V EF

INGREDIENTS
FOR THE DIP
1 x 400g can of cannellini beans, drained, rinsed

1 clove garlic

1 lemon, juiced

1 tbsp olive oil

salt, to taste

TO SERVE
1 tsp paprika

1/4 cup cucumber, finely diced

1/4 cup roasted peppers, finely diced (see note)

1 1/2 tbsp pine nuts, toasted

25g feta cheese

NOTES
I like to use jarred roasted red peppers for this recipe to make it quick and easy, but you can roast your own capsicum at home.

METHOD
1. Add the beans, garlic, lemon juice and oil to a food processor and blitz until smooth and creamy, adding more juice and oil if needed. Season to taste with salt.
2. Spread dip out on a serving platter and lightly sprinkle on paprika.
3. Top with cucumber, roasted peppers and toasted pine nuts, leaving a 1cm border. Crumble over feta cheese.
4. Serve with tortilla or pita chips.

Fresh Tomato Salsa (Pico de Gallo)

I love to simply serve this salsa with tortilla chips and guacamole, but it also makes the perfect addition to taco night! Another of my favourite ways to have it is to spoon it on top of grilled chicken with sweet chilli sauce - absolutely delicious!

 PREPTIME: 5-10 MIN

 **SERVES:** 4 PEOPLE

     GF DF V EF NF VG

INGREDIENTS
2 medium tomatoes
1/4 red onion
1 lime, juiced
1 small chilli (optional)
salt & pepper, to taste

METHOD
1. Dice the tomatoes, red onion and chilli and add to a serving bowl. Add lime juice and season to taste with salt and pepper.
2. Mix together thoroughly to incorporate. This salsa can be served with corn or tortilla chips, served over grilled chicken or in tacos, burritos or nachos.

NOTES
This salsa is great served with 'Cheats' Tortilla Chips (p. 71).

71 'Cheats' Tortilla Chips

Crunchy, salty and easy homemade baked tortilla chips are perfect to snack on with salsa or guacamole! With only four ingredients, these cheats tortilla chips only take 15 minutes to make!

PREPTIME: 5 MIN

COOKTIME: 10 MIN

SERVES: 4 PEOPLE

INGREDIENTS

2 large flour tortillas
2 tbsp oil
salt & pepper, to taste

NOTES

These chips are great served with Chilli Con Carne (p. 101), Fresh Tomato Salsa (Pico de Gallo) (p. 69), Beetroot & Pistachio Dip (p. 57), Spinach & Feta Dip (p. 59), Roasted Capsicum Bean Dip (p. 61) and Mediterranean Layered White Bean Dip (p. 67)

METHOD

1. Preheat oven to 180°C and line a baking tray with baking paper.
2. Drizzle oil over tortillas, rubbing over both sides. Season each side with salt and pepper and cut each tortilla into 16 triangles.
3. Spread out on baking tray and bake for 10 mins or until golden and crispy.

73 Lime & Black Pepper Potato Chips

If you're looking for a healthy, but delicious version of store bought potato chips, then you've come to the right place! These baked chips are just as satisfying as the regular fried alternatives and are so easy and fun to make! These are a salty snack that you don't have to feel guilty about!

 PREPTIME: 5-10 MIN

 COOKTIME: 15-20 MIN

 **SERVES:** 2 PEOPLE

     GF DF V EF NF VG

INGREDIENTS

2 x medium russet potatoes (see note)
2 tbsp olive oil
juice & zest of 1 lime
freshly cracked black pepper
salt, to taste

NOTES
1. Any kind of potatoes can be substituted, even sweet potatoes.
2. This recipe can be made with either peeled or washed skin-on potatoes.

METHOD

1. Preheat oven to 200°C and line a baking tray with baking paper. Wash potatoes and slice into 1/8 inch slices.
2. Add to a bowl with oil, lime juice and zest, salt and pepper. Toss to combine. Arrange potato slices on baking tray and bake for 15-20 mins or until golden and crispy. Enjoy!

CHAPTER 03

Sides

77 Warm Zucchini, Feta & Pine Nut Salad

This warm zucchini salad is amazing with any meal...It goes wonderfully with steak or grilled chicken and is a great way to add a little flavour to a simple vegetable!

 PREPTIME: 5 MIN

 COOKTIME: 10 MIN

 **MAKES:** 4 SIDE SALADS

INGREDIENTS

2 medium zucchini
1 tbsp oil
salt & pepper, to taste
1/2 lemon, juiced
2 tbsp pine nuts, toasted
50g feta cheese

NOTES
Try serving this salad with Lemon & Paprika Baked Chicken (p. 149)

METHOD

1. Place a large frying pan on medium heat. Slice zucchini into rounds and drizzle with oil. Season with salt and pepper and add to pan.
2. Grill zucchini until golden brown on both sides then remove from pan and place on serving platter.
3. Drizzle with lemon juice and scatter over pine nuts and crumbled feta.
4. Serve warm as a light side.

"Before juicing a lemon, roll it on a bench, whilst pushing down on it to release more juice"

81 Easy Greek Salad

This Easy Greek Salad recipe is made with only a handful of ingredients and is so quick and simple to make! The salad combines fresh cherry tomatoes, cucumber, red onion, feta cheese and kalamata olives with a tasty vinaigrette for an easy side dish for summer.

TIME: 5 MIN

MAKES: 4 SIDE SALADS

GF V NF EF

INGREDIENTS

FOR THE SALAD
10 cherry tomatoes, halved
1/3 cucumber, sliced
1/4 red onion, sliced
8 kalamata olives, pitted
40g feta cheese

FOR THE DRESSING
1 tbsp olive oil
1/4 lemon, juiced
1 tsp red wine vinegar
1/2 tsp dijon mustard
1 clove garlic, minced

METHOD

1. Combine tomatoes, cucumber, onion and olives in a bowl and crumble over feta.
2. Add all dressing ingredients to a small bowl and whisk to combine. Pour over salad and toss through to combine. Serve.

NOTES
Try serving this salad with Greek Chicken Skewers (p. 133)

Sautéed Leeks with Garlic & Chilli Oil

These sautéed leeks are a simple and delicious side dish that's perfect with steak or fish. The chilli & garlic oil add flavour and a hint of heat which really makes this a winning side.

 PREPTIME: 5 MIN

 COOKTIME: 10-15 MIN

 **SERVES:** 4 SIDES

INGREDIENTS

FOR THE LEEKS
2 leeks
1 tbsp oil
2 tbsp butter
1 clove garlic, thinly sliced
salt & pepper, to taste

FOR THE OIL
1 tsp dried chilli flakes
1/4 cup oil
1 clove garlic, finely diced

METHOD

1. To prepare the leeks, trim 1cm off of each end of the leeks and wash thoroughly to remove any dirt. Cut leeks in half lengthwise.
2. Heat oil and butter in a large frying pan on medium-high heat. Add leeks, cut side down, along with garlic. Season with salt and pepper.
3. Sauté for 5 mins or until leeks are golden brown. Flip and continue to cook until leeks are tender and golden on all sides. Remove leeks and garlic from the pan.
4. Meanwhile, for the oil, place chilli flakes in a small heatproof bowl and set aside.
5. Heat oil in a small saucepan on high heat. Once hot, add garlic and fry until garlic turns golden, about 2 mins.
6. Carefully pour oil over chilli flakes. Spoon chilli oil over leeks and serve.

Homemade Battered Onion Rings

Onion Rings are a classic side dish that you often associate with a pub or burger place...but they're incredibly easy to make yourself at home! These onion rings offer a twist on a classic with a touch of cayenne pepper for an added kick...It makes all the difference.

 PREPTIME: 5 MIN

 COOKTIME: 10-15 MIN

 **SERVES:** 4 SIDES

INGREDIENTS

- vegetable oil, for frying
- 1/4 cup plain flour
- 1/2 tsp baking powder
- 1/2 tsp salt (plus extra, to serve)
- 1/2 tsp cayenne pepper
- 1 egg, beaten
- 100ml water
- 1 onion, sliced into rings
- chives (for garnish, optional)

NOTES
1. To make this recipe easier, try using a mandoline to slice the onions.
2. Try serving these onion rings with Beef & Horseradish Sliders (p. 113)

METHOD

1. Heat oil to 180°C in a medium heavy-based pan or dutch oven, making sure it is no more than ⅓ full.
2. Meanwhile, whisk together flour, baking powder, salt and cayenne pepper in a medium mixing bowl. Whisk in egg and water until well combined.
3. Dip onion slices into the batter, a few at a time, until all are evenly coated. Deep-fry in batches until crispy and golden brown, about 2-3 mins. Remove with a slotted spoon and place on paper towel to drain. Repeat with remaining onions and batter.
4. Season to taste with salt and garnish with chives. Serve.

87 Garlic Buttered Grilled Corn Cobs

These Garlic Buttered Grilled Corn Cobs are an easy and tasty side dish that is perfect for the summer BBQ! These corn cobs can be grilled on the barbecue or in a frying pan with a delicious and simple garlic butter sauce.

PREPTIME: 5 MIN

COOKTIME: 10-15 MIN

SERVES: 4 SIDES

INGREDIENTS
2 tbsp butter
1/2 tsp dried chilli flakes (optional)
1 clove garlic, finely diced
1 tbsp oil
2 whole corn cobs
fresh parsley, to serve (optional)

METHOD
1. Place butter in a small heatproof bowl and microwave until melted, about 30 seconds. Add chilli flakes and garlic and stir to combine.
2. Add oil to a large frying pan or barbecue on high heat along with corn. Brush corn with butter using a pastry brush and cook, turning often and basting occasionally for 10-15 mins or until tender.
3. Cut corn cobs in half and garnish with parsley.

NOTES
1. These corn cobs can be made on the BBQ or in a frying pan.
2. Try serving these corn cobs with Lemon & Paprika Baked Chicken (p. 149)

89 Stuffed Baked Potatoes Three Ways - Cheesy Bacon

Stuffed potatoes are the ultimate side dish for just about any meal, from steak to chicken and everything in between. That's why in this book I'm doing three different types. And the first one on the list - Cheesy Bacon - is one of my favourites!

 PREPTIME: 5 MIN

 COOKTIME: 1 HOUR 5 MIN

 **SERVES:** 4 SIDES

INGREDIENTS

FOR THE POTATOES
4 medium russet potatoes
2 tbsp oil
salt & pepper, to taste
1 tbsp butter
1/4 cup grated cheese
30g bacon, diced

TO SERVE
1/4 cup sour cream
2 tbsp fresh chives, diced

METHOD

1. Wash potatoes and, using a fork, stab 5-6 times. Drizzle with oil and season with salt and pepper. Place in an air fryer or oven at 200°C and cook for 55-60 mins or until fork-tender.
2. Carefully remove potatoes from air fryer and cut in half. Scoop out the insides of the potatoes into a bowl, leaving a 1cm edge.
3. Add butter and salt, to taste, and mash with a fork until smooth. Scoop back into potato skins and top with grated cheese and bacon. Air fry or bake for 5-10 mins or until cheese is golden.
4. Remove from air fryer or oven and serve with sour cream and chives.

91. Stuffed Baked Potatoes Three Ways – Spinach & Pumpkin

This delicious Spinach & Pumpkin Baked Potato is the perfect vegetarian side dish! It's both healthy and hearty and loaded with all the good stuff.

 PREPTIME: 5 MIN

 COOKTIME: 65 MIN

 **SERVES:** 4 SIDES

 GF | NF | EF | V

INGREDIENTS

FOR THE POTATOES
4 medium russet potatoes
2 tbsp oil
salt & pepper, to taste
2 cups baby spinach
1 cup boiled pumpkin, mashed
1/4 cup grated cheese

METHOD

1. Wash potatoes and, using a fork, stab 5-6 times. Drizzle with oil and season with salt and pepper. Place in air fryer or oven at 200°C and cook for 55-60 mins or until fork-tender.
2. Carefully remove potatoes from air fryer and cut in half. Scoop out the insides of the potatoes into a medium bowl, leaving a 1cm edge. Set aside.
3. Add spinach to a large frying pan on medium heat and cook until wilted, about 2-3 mins. Remove from pan and add to potatoes along with pumpkin. Season to taste with salt and pepper and stir together until well combined.
4. Spoon mixture into potato skins and top with cheese. Bake for 5 mins in air fryer or oven or until cheese is golden. Serve.

93 Stuffed Baked Potatoes Three Ways - Sour Cream & Chives

The third and last stuffed potato recipe is arguably one of the best. These Sour Cream & Chives Stuffed Potatoes are a delicious side that are super simple to whip up any day of the week.

PREPTIME: 5 MIN

COOKTIME: 65 MIN

SERVES: 4 SIDES

INGREDIENTS

FOR THE POTATOES
4 medium russet potatoes
2 tbsp oil
salt & pepper, to taste
1 tbsp butter
1/2 tsp onion powder
1/4 cup parmesan cheese

TO SERVE
1/4 cup sour cream
2 tbsp fresh chives, diced

METHOD

1. Wash potatoes and, using a fork, stab 5-6 times. Drizzle with oil and season with salt and pepper. Place in air fryer or oven and cook at 200°C for 55-60 mins or until fork-tender.
2. Carefully remove potatoes from air fryer and cut in half. Scoop out the inside of the potatoes into a bowl, leaving a 1cm edge.
3. Add butter and onion powder to potatoes and season to taste with salt and pepper. Roughly mash with a fork until combined.
4. Spoon mixture back into potatoes, top each one with parmesan cheese and return to the air fryer or oven for 3-5 mins or until cheese has melted.
5. Remove from oven and top each one with sour cream and chives. Serve.

Apple, Rocket & Pine Nut Salad

This Apple, Rocket & Pine Nut Salad is the perfect combination of sweet and savoury! The fresh sweetness of the apple is balanced with the peppery rocket, and the nutty flavour of the pine nuts just sends this salad to the next level! Yum!

 PREPTIME: 5-10 MIN

 COOKTIME: 2 MIN

 **SERVES:** 4 SIDES

INGREDIENTS

FOR THE SALAD

2 tbsp pine nuts

1 green apple, sliced

2 cups rocket leaves

50g shaved parmesan cheese

FOR THE DRESSING

3 tbsp olive oil

1 1/2 tbsp balsamic vinegar

1 tsp dijon mustard

1/3 tsp minced garlic

METHOD

1. Place a frying pan on medium heat and gently toast pine nuts, being very careful to keep an eye on them. Remove and set aside.
2. Add apple to a medium bowl along with rocket, parmesan and pine nuts.
3. For the dressing, combine ingredients in a jar or small container with a lid and shake until well combined.
4. Drizzle the dressing over the salad and toss until evenly coated. Serve.

"who said salad has to be boring?"

CHAPTER 04
Main Meals

101 Chilli Con Carne with 'Cheats' Tortilla Chips

This Chilli Con Carne recipe is the best thing for any Winter. A delicious stew of beef mince, tomatoes and a tasty combination of spices, this easy dish is the perfect weeknight dinner.

 PREPTIME: 5-10 MIN

 COOKTIME: 50 MIN

 **SERVES:** 4 PEOPLE

 DF EF NF

INGREDIENTS

FOR THE CHILLI
1 tbsp oil
1 onion, diced
2 cloves garlic, finely diced
1/2 red capsicum, diced
500g beef mince
1 x 400g can diced tomatoes
2 tsp tomato paste
1/2 tsp cayenne pepper
2 tsp paprika
2 tsp cumin
2 tsp chilli powder
500ml beef stock
2 tbsp worcestershire sauce
salt & pepper, to taste
rice, to serve

FOR THE CHIPS
2 tortillas
1 tbsp oil
salt & pepper, to taste

METHOD

1. Heat oil in a large saucepan o medium/high heat and cook the onions, garlic and capsicum for 4-5 mins or until onions are soft.
2. Add the beef and cook, stirring occasionally until browned, breaking any large chunks wit a wooden spoon.
3. Add the tomatoes, tomato paste, spices, stock and worcestershire sauce and stir until well combined. Season to taste with salt and pepper an bring to a gentle simmer. Coo uncovered, stirring occasionally, for 30-45 mins or until the liquid has reduced by half.
4. Meanwhile, for the chips, preheat the oven to 180°C. Rub each tortilla with oil and season both sides with salt and pepper. Cut each tortilla into 16 pieces and cook for 5-1 mins or until golden.
5. Serve Chilli Con Carne with ric and tortilla chips.

NOTES
Try adding a 400g tin of kidney beans to this recipe!

103 Mini Chicken Curry Pot Pies

Ahhh...chicken pot pies! I just love the smell of the crispy golden puff pastry filling the kitchen as they cook. Sometimes a good pie is all you need on a cold Winter's night – especially a mini chicken pot pie! And the best thing about this recipe? It is ridiculously cheap to make! And I mean cheap.

 PREPTIME: 5 MIN

 COOKTIME: 40 MIN

 MAKES: 4 PIES

 NF

INGREDIENTS

2 x 165g sheets frozen puff pastry, thawed
1 onion, diced
1 clove garlic, finely diced
1 tbsp oil
1-2 tbsp butter
2 tsp plain flour
1/4 cup heavy cream
1/2 cup chicken stock
1 cup shredded roast chicken
1 tsp fresh thyme, diced
1 tsp curry powder
1 tbsp soy sauce
salt & pepper, to taste
1 egg, beaten

NOTES

1. If you don't have any leftover chicken on hand, just bake a large seasoned breast in the oven at 200°C for 20-30 minutes!
2. You can easily make this into a whole family pot pie if you like! Just add one sheet of puff pastry to a large pie dish, add filling and cover with another sheet, brush with egg and bake!

METHOD

1. Preheat oven to 180°C and cut each sheet of pastry into four even squares. Set aside.
2. Sauté onion and garlic in oil on medium heat until tender. Meanwhile, butter four ramekins and line with pastry and set aside.
3. Add flour to onions and garlic and cook, stirring constantly, for 1 minute. Add cream and stock and stir. Add chicken, thyme, curry powder, soy sauce and season to taste with salt and pepper. Simmer until thickened.
4. Remove from heat and divide evenly between prepared ramekins. Add pastry on top, trimming off the excess if desired, and squeeze the edges to seal. Brush with beaten egg and cook for 20-30 mins or until pastry is golden.

105 Tuna Patties & Homemade Chips

This recipe is my take on a budget fish & chips. The tuna patties utilise basic pantry staples to make an easy, cheap and satisfying meal! The homemade chips and tartare sauce take this recipe from budget basics to homemade takeaway!

PREPTIME: 10-15 MIN

COOKTIME: 45-50 MIN

SERVES: 4 PEOPLE

NF

INGREDIENTS

FOR THE PATTIES
2 medium potatoes, peeled and washed
50ml milk
2 tsp butter
3 x 95g tins tuna in water
2 cloves garlic, finely diced
1 tbsp dried chives
1 tbsp lemon juice
1 egg
1/4 cup plain flour
salt & pepper, to taste
oil, for frying

FOR THE CHIPS
2 medium potatoes, washed
1 tbsp oil
salt, to taste

FOR THE SAUCE
1/2 cup mayonnaise
1 tbsp lemon juice
1 gherkin, finely diced
1 tsp capers, finely diced
1/2 tsp dried dill

METHOD

1. Roughly chop potatoes into equal sized pieces and boil until fork tender. Remove from saucepan, rinse and drain. Add to a bowl along with milk and butter. Mash until smooth.
2. Drain tuna and add to potatoes along with garlic, chives, lemon juice, egg and flour. Season with salt and pepper and mix until thoroughly combined.
3. Take a small amount of mixture and roll into a golf ball sized ball. Push down to flatten slightly and repeat with remaining mixture.
4. Coat the bottom of a large frying pan with oil and heat to medium high. Fry patties in batches until golden brown, about 3 mins on each side.
5. Place tuna patties in air fryer and cook for 5 mins at 200°C to crisp up. Season with salt and set aside.
6. For the chips, cut potatoes into 1cm thick slices, then cut into 1cm thick chips. Add to a bowl and coat with oil. Air fry for 30-40 mins or until golden brown. Remove from air fryer and season with salt. Set aside.
7. For the sauce, combine all ingredients and stir thoroughly to combine. Serve with tuna patties, chips and lemon wedges.

107 Slow Cooker Beef Ragu with Fettuccine

This is probably my new favourite pasta dish and it couldn't be easier to make! All you have to do is dice up the vegetables and place them along with everything else in the slow cooker. Set the timer and wait for the magic to happen!

PREPTIME: 5-10 MIN

COOKTIME: 6 HOURS 30 MIN

SERVES: 6 PEOPLE

NF EF DF

INGREDIENTS

1 tbsp oil
1 carrot, finely diced
1 celery stalk, finely diced
1 onion, finely diced
2 cloves garlic, diced
750g chuck steak
700ml passata
500ml beef stock
1/4 tsp dried oregano
2 bay leaves
1 tbsp cornflour
2 tbsp water
salt & pepper, to taste
500g dried fettuccine pasta

METHOD

1. Add oil, carrots, celery, onion, garlic and beef to slow cooker along with passata, stock, oregano and bay leaves.
2. In a small bowl, whisk flour and water thoroughly to combine and add to slow cooker. Season to taste with salt and pepper and stir to combine.
3. Cover and cook on low heat for 6 hours. Remove lid and sauté, uncovered, for 30 mins. Remove and discard bay leaves.
4. Remove beef and shred using two forks. Return to slow cooker and stir to combine.
5. Meanwhile, bring a large pot of water to the boil and season generously with salt. Cook pasta according to packet instructions. Drain.
6. Toss pasta with sauce and divide between bowls. Serve.

NOTES
If your slow cooker doesn't have a 'sauté' setting that allows it to boil, then simply transfer to a large saucepan!

109 Chicken Maryland Traybake

Traybakes have to be one of the easiest things to make for dinner! All you have to do is throw everything on a tray and, well; bake it. Simple. In this recipe I'm using chicken marylands, one of my favourite cuts of meat! Delicious!

 PREPTIME: 5-10 MIN

 COOKTIME: 45-50 MIN

 SERVES: 4 PEOPLE

INGREDIENTS

- 4 chicken marylands
- 2 tbsp lemon juice
- 1 tsp paprika
- 1 tsp garlic salt
- 4 chat potatoes, washed
- 1/3 red capsicum
- 1 red onion
- 1 tbsp oil
- salt and pepper, to taste
- fresh parsley, to serve (optional)

METHOD

1. Preheat oven to 180°C and line a large baking tray with baking paper. Place chicken on tray, drizzle with lemon juice and season with paprika and garlic salt.
2. Chop each potato in half, roughly chop capsicum and cut onion into wedges. Scatter vegetables around the chicken and drizzle with oil. Season with salt and pepper and bake for 45-50 mins or until chicken is cooked through. Garnish with parsley and serve.

113 Beef & Horseradish Sliders with Caramelised Onions

These homemade Beef Sliders are an easy weeknight treat! Served with a special horseradish cream sauce and caramelised onions, they're perfect for BBQ's, grilling and family dinners!

 PREPTIME: 10 MIN

 COOKTIME: 20 MIN

 MAKES: 6 BURGERS

INGREDIENTS

FOR THE PATTIES
500g beef mince
1/2 onion, diced
1 clove garlic, finely diced
1 tsp wholegrain mustard
1 egg
1/4 cup breadcrumbs
salt & pepper, to taste
1 tbsp oil

FOR THE ONIONS
1 large onion, sliced
1 tbsp oil
2 tsp brown sugar
1 1/2 tbsp balsamic vinegar

FOR THE SAUCE
1/2 cup sour cream
1 1/2 tsp cream-styled prepared horseradish

TO SERVE
6 slices cheddar cheese
rocket or lettuce
tomatoes, sliced
6 slider buns, lightly toasted

METHOD

1. For the patties, combine all the ingredients in a large bowl with your hands and separate into 6 even patties.
2. Add 1 tbsp oil to a large pan or grill on high heat and cook on both sides until nicely coloured and cooked through. Place a slice of cheese on each patty and allow to melt.
3. Meanwhile, for the caramelised onions, gently sauté onions in oil on a low heat until slightly softened and add sugar and balsamic vinegar. Let cook, stirring occasionally, for 15-20 mins. Remove from heat.
4. To make the sauce, combine sour cream and prepared horseradish in a small bowl and set aside.
5. To assemble the sliders, place rocket and sliced tomato on a bun and top with patty. Place the onions on top of the meat and dollop the horseradish cream sauce on top. Devour.

115 Chicken & Vegetable Soup

This homemade Chicken and Vegetable Soup is an easy and simple classic for Winter! Loaded with shredded chicken, garlic, simple vegetables and seasonings, this is a comforting broth of goodness! It's also a healthy and light dinner option that is sure to help you feel better when you're sick!

PREPTIME: 10 MIN

COOKTIME: 1 HOUR 30 MIN

SERVES: 6 PEOPLE

INGREDIENTS

1 tbsp oil
2 cloves garlic, finely diced
1 onion, chopped
2 carrots, sliced
2 celery stalks, diced
1 leek, chopped
1 L chicken stock
250ml water
4 chicken thighs (about 500g)
2 bay leaves
1/2 tsp fresh thyme
salt & pepper, to taste
1 cup green beans, cut to desired length
crusty bread, to serve

NOTES

1. Add in some cooked pasta to make a homemade chicken noodle soup.
2. This soup recipe is gluten-free if you serve it with gluten-free bread or no bread at all.

METHOD

1. Add oil, garlic, onion, carrot, celery and leek to a large saucepan over medium heat and sautè until vegetables are soft and tender.
2. Pour in chicken stock and water and bring to a gentle simmer before adding whole chicken thighs, bay leaves, thyme, salt and pepper. Cover with a lid and cook for 1 hour.
3. Remove chicken and using two forks, shred. Return to saucepan along with beans. Check for seasoning and simmer, covered, for 5-10 mins or until beans are tender. Serve with fresh, crusty bread.

117 Roast Leg of Lamb with Mint Sauce

Everyone loves a good roast dinner, and it doesn't get much better than a roast leg of lamb! And this recipe is the perfect dish for any occasion. Served with a homemade mint sauce and roasted onions, this roast lamb will be a family favourite.

PREPTIME: 10 MIN

COOKTIME: 1 HOUR 15 MIN

SERVES: 8 PEOPLE

GF DF NF EF

INGREDIENTS

1 lemon, juiced
2 tbsp lemon zest
2 cloves garlic, finely diced
1/2 tsp ground cumin
2 tbsp honey
1/2 tbsp brown sugar
2 tbsp fresh chives, diced
5 rosemary sprigs
2kg leg of lamb
salt & pepper, to taste
2 onions, quartered

FOR THE MINT SAUCE
3/4 cup fresh mint leaves, finely chopped
2 tsp sugar
1/4 cup boiling water
1/2 cup white vinegar

METHOD

1. Preheat oven to 180°C and line a baking tray with baking paper. Set aside.
2. In a small bowl, add lemon juice, zest, garlic, cumin, honey, sugar, chives and 1 sprig of rosemary, roughly chopped and stir to combine.
3. Place lamb on prepared baking tray and cover with marinade. Season with salt and pepper. Place remaining rosemary sprigs on top of lamb and place onions around lamb.
4. Cook for 1 hour 15 mins for medium or until cooked to your liking.
5. For the sauce, add mint to a heatproof jug or bowl along with sugar. Pour over boiling water and stir. Add vinegar, stir to combine and serve with lamb.

when life hands you lemons make ~~lemonade~~ marinade!

121 Crumbed Cheese & Broccoli Stuffed Chicken

Cheese & Broccoli Stuffed Chicken Breasts are the perfect comfort food! The delicious combination of broccoli and cheese works so well with baked crumbed chicken for an easy dinner the whole family will love!

 PREPTIME: 20 MIN

 COOKTIME: 35-40 MIN

 **SERVES: 8 PEOPLE**

 NF

INGREDIENTS

FOR THE FILLING
1 small head broccoli
60g butter
1/3 cup plain flour
500ml milk
1 cup grated cheese

FOR THE CHICKEN
8 chicken breasts
1 cup breadcrumbs
2 eggs, beaten
1/2 cup plain flour
1/2 tsp salt
pepper, to taste
oil, for frying

METHOD

1. Preheat oven to 180°C and line a baking tray with baking paper. Set aside.
2. Roughly chop broccoli into florets and blitz in a food processor until fine rice-sized pieces are formed, scraping the edge of the bowl as needed. Set aside.
3. Place a saucepan on medium heat and add butter. Allow to melt before adding flour and stirring with a whisk until combined. Pour in milk and whisk constantly, until thick. Remove from heat and add cheese. Stir to combine and allow to cool slightly before stirring through broccoli.
4. To stuff the chicken, make an incision with a sharp knife from just before the top of the breast to just before the bottom. Use your fingers to form a pocket inside the breast. Be sure to stop half an inch from the ends and sides. Repeat with remaining breasts.
5. Spoon 1-2 tbsp of mixture into each chicken breast and secure with toothpicks if needed.
6. In three separate shallow bowls, add breadcrumbs, eggs and flour. Season breadcrumbs with salt and pepper.
7. Dip each chicken breast into flour, then into egg and finally in the breadcrumbs, making sure each one is evenly coated. Shallow fry breasts on both sides until golden and place on prepared baking tray. Cook in the oven for 25-30 mins or until cooked through.

Juicy crumbed chicken stuffed with a cheesy broccoli sauce! Delish!

125 Asian Beef & Noodle Soup

A delicious and flavoursome Asian inspired broth made with aromatic spices, rice noodles, pak choi and thinly sliced steak makes this recipe a truly comforting soup for any occasion!

 PREPTIME: 5 MIN

 COOKTIME: 35-40 MIN

 **SERVES:** 6 PEOPLE

   DF NF EF

INGREDIENTS

FOR THE BROTH
1 tbsp oil
2 cloves garlic, finely diced
1L beef stock
1 tsp fish sauce
2 tsp oyster sauce
2 tbsp soy sauce
juice of 1/2 lime
1/4 tsp chilli flakes
1/4 tsp ground ginger
salt & pepper, to taste

TO SERVE
500g raw rump steak
200g thin rice noodles
6 baby pak choi
1 tsp sesame seeds

METHOD

1. Gently heat oil in a dutch oven or large saucepan on medium heat and add garlic. Sauté until slightly golden and add stock, fish sauce, oyster sauce, soy sauce, lime juice, chilli flakes and ginger.

2. Bring to a gentle simmer and allow to cook, covered, for 30 mins. Season to taste with salt and pepper. Meanwhile, slice steak into paper thin strips and set aside.

3. Submerge noodles and pak choi in the broth and cook for 5 mins or until pak choi is tender. To serve, divide noodles and pak choi into six bowls and add raw beef. Ladle hot broth over beef to cook through. Sprinkle over sesame seeds and serve.

Crispy Air Fryer Chicken Legs

127

These Crispy Air Fryer Chicken Legs are quick, easy and so much healthier than regular fried chicken...The whole family will be sure to love this drumstick recipe!

PREPTIME: 5 MIN

COOKTIME: 30 MIN

SERVES: 4 PEOPLE

GF DF EF NF

INGREDIENTS

1 1/2 tbsp garlic salt
2 tsp paprika
2 tsp onion powder
pepper. to taste
3 tbsp oil
8 chicken drumsticks

NOTES
This recipe can easily be made with chicken wings or thighs as well!

METHOD

1. In a small bowl, combine garlic salt, paprika, onion powder and pepper. Set aside.
2. Lay chicken legs out on a large plate and drizzle with oil. Sprinkle spice mix over chicken and rub all over to evenly coat.
3. Place chicken in air fryer and cook at 200°C for 30 mins or until cooked through. Serve.

"serve these legs with salad or eat them on their own"

To cook good food does not mean it has to be fancy. The best meals come from the heart.

131 Ribeye Steak with Mushroom Sauce

Steak is one of those things that you look forward to eating when you go out for dinner, whether you're dining at a 5-star restaurant or the local pub. But once you try this method of cooking, you'll be having delicious, butter basted steak at home!

PREPTIME: 5 MIN

COOKTIME: 10-15 MIN

SERVES: 4 PEOPLE

INGREDIENTS

FOR THE STEAK
- 1 tbsp oil
- 2 tbsp butter
- 4 ribeye steaks
- salt & pepper, to taste
- 3 sprigs rosemary
- 2 cloves garlic, peeled

FOR THE SAUCE
- 3 tbsp butter
- 2 cloves garlic, finely diced
- 8 button mushrooms, sliced
- salt & pepper, to taste
- 3/4 cup milk
- 1 tbsp cornflour
- 2 tbsp water

NOTES
1. This recipe is for medium-rare steaks, however you can adjust the cooking times to suit your own preferences.
2. Try serving this dish with some Homemade Battered Onion Rings (p. 85)

METHOD

1. Add oil and butter to a large frying pan on medium heat. Season steaks with salt and pepper and add to hot pan, two at a time.
2. Cook for three mins and flip. Add rosemary and whole garlic cloves to the pan. Spoon the melted butter over the steaks and cook for 3 mins. Remove from pan and allow to rest for at least 5 mins. Repeat with remaining steaks.
3. For the sauce, add butter, garlic and mushrooms to a medium saucepan over medium heat. Cook, stirring occasionally, until mushrooms are golden and start to stick to the pan. Season with salt and pepper and add milk.
4. Combine cornflour and water in a small bowl and add to sauce. Stir through and allow to simmer until thickened, about 3-5 mins. Serve with your favourite sides.

133 Greek Chicken Skewers

Let's talk skewers. I love them. LOVE them. They're honestly my favourite thing to throw on the barbecue in the summer time and the first thing I always go to. And this easy recipe is perfect for the whole family!

 PREPTIME: 15-20 MIN

 COOKTIME: 10-15 MIN

 SERVES: 4 PEOPLE

INGREDIENTS

FOR THE MARINADE
1/2 cup lemon juice
3 cloves garlic, finely diced
2 tbsp honey
2 tsp fresh parsley, finely chopped (see notes)
1 tsp fresh thyme, finely chopped (see notes)
3 tbsp olive oil, plus extra for grilling
salt & pepper, to taste

FOR THE SKEWERS
4 chicken thighs, cut into 1 1/2 inch pieces
1 red capsicum, cut into 1 1/2 inch pieces
1/2 red onion, cut into 1 1/2 inch pieces
wooden skewers, soaked in water for 30 mins

NOTES
1. If you can't get fresh herbs, just substitute with 1/3 tsp of dried thyme and 2/3 tsp of dried parsley
2. Try serving these skewers with an Easy Greek Salad (p. 81)

METHOD
1. For the marinade, add lemon juice, garlic, honey, herbs, oil, salt and pepper to a small bowl and stir to combine. Set aside.
2. Thread chicken onto skewers, alternating with capsicum and onion. Repeat with remaining ingredients.
3. Add to a large container with a secure lid and pour over marinade, tossing to evenly coat. Place in the fridge and marinate for around 2 hours, tossing again at 1 hour.
4. Grill skewers for 3-4 mins on each side or until chicken is cooked through and juices run clear.

135 Fettuccine Carbonara

Now before we dive in, I'm just going to say that this recipe isn't the most traditional Italian meal out there....most Carbonara recipes don't call for cream. The creaminess comes solely from the egg yolks, but I personally think the cream just makes it so much better!

 PREPTIME: 10 MIN

 COOKTIME: 10-15 MIN

 SERVES: 4 PEOPLE

INGREDIENTS

250g dried fettuccine pasta
2 eggs, beaten
300ml thickened cream
1/2 cup parmesan cheese, grated
1 tsp garlic salt
pepper, to taste
1 tbsp oil
2 cloves garlic, finely diced
fresh parsley, for garnish (optional)
extra parmesan cheese, to serve

METHOD

1. Bring a large pot of water to the boil and season generously with salt. Add pasta and cook according to packet directions.
2. Meanwhile, combine eggs, cream, cheese, garlic salt and pepper in a bowl and set aside.
3. Add oil to a large frying pan on medium-high heat and gently sauté garlic until golden.
4. Add pasta and remove frying pan from heat. Pour in cream mixture and stir to combine. Allow to sit for 2-3 mins, stirring until slightly thickened. Serve with fresh parsley and grated parmesan cheese.

NOTES

Keep in mind that the parmesan cheese is quite salty so be mindful when seasoning.

137 Butter Chicken

This homemade Butter Chicken recipe is an easy and comforting curry that will transport you to your favourite Indian restaurant! Made with chicken thighs, fresh garlic and spices, this Butter Chicken is a flavoursome dish that's ready in 45 minutes!

 PREPTIME: 5-10 MIN

 COOKTIME: 30-35 MIN

 SERVES: 4 PEOPLE

INGREDIENTS

FOR THE CURRY
- 6 tbsp butter, divided
- 1kg chicken thighs, cut into 1" chunks
- 1 onion, diced
- 3 garlic cloves, minced
- 1 tbsp garam masala
- 1 tbsp ground ginger
- 1 tsp chilli powder
- 1 tsp ground cumin
- 1/2 tsp cayenne pepper
- 1/4 tsp sugar
- 2 cups passata
- 2 cups thickened cream
- salt & pepper, to taste

TO SERVE
- basmati rice
- naan bread
- papadams (optional)

METHOD

1. Add 2 tbsp of butter to a large skillet over medium-high heat and, working in batches, cook the chicken until browned. Set aside.
2. Melt another 2 tbsp of butter in the pan over medium heat. Add the onion, and cook for 2-3 mins or until beginning to soften. Add the garlic, garam masala, ginger, chilli powder, cumin, cayenne and sugar. Stir to combine, and cook for about 45 seconds before adding the passata.
3. Bring the sauce to a simmer and let cook for 5 mins before adding in the cream. Bring the mixture back to a simmer, return the chicken to the pan and let simmer for 10-15 mins. Keep the heat low here and don't boil it too hard.
4. Stir in the remaining 2 tbsp of butter and season with salt and pepper, to taste. Serve with rice, naan bead or papadams.

BUTTER IS THE QUINTESSENTIAL INGREDIENT THAT MAKES ANYTHING TASTE AMAZING.

Savoury Mince & Coleslaw Loaded Potatoes

I love loaded baked potatoes! So for this book, I'm bringing you my favourite way to make them! These Savoury Mince & Coleslaw Potatoes are such a delicious and satisfying meal, you'll soon have them on your weekly rotation.

PREPTIME: 10-15 MIN

COOKTIME: 1 HOUR 5 MIN

SERVES: 4 PEOPLE

NF EF

INGREDIENTS

FOR THE POTATOES
4 medium russet potatoes
2 tbsp oil
salt & pepper, to taste

FOR THE MINCE
1 tbsp oil
1/2 onion, diced
1 clove garlic, finely diced
500g beef mince
2 tbsp worcestershire sauce
2 tbsp gravy powder
3 tbsp tomato sauce
300ml beef stock

FOR THE COLESLAW
1 cup red cabbage, thinly sliced
1 small carrot, grated
1/4 cup diced capsicum
1/4 cup mayonnaise
1/2 tsp dijon mustard
1/3 tsp honey
1 tsp chives, diced

TO SERVE
1/2 cup cheese, grated
4 tbsp sour cream

METHOD

1. Wash potatoes, and using a fork, stab each one 5-6 times. Drizzle with oil and season with salt and pepper. Place in air fryer or oven and cook at 200°C for 55-60 mins or until fork-tender.

2. Meanwhile, heat oil in a large frying pan and sauté onion until tender. Add garlic and mince. Cook, stirring with a wooden spoon to break up mince, for 6 to 8 mins or until browned. Add worcestershire sauce, gravy powder, tomato sauce and stock and stir to combine. Allow to simmer until reduced, about 10-15 mins.

3. For the coleslaw, add cabbage, carrot and capsicum to a bowl. In a separate small bowl, add mayonnaise, mustard, honey and chives and stir to combine. Pour over cabbage mixture and toss to coat evenly.

4. To serve, slice open each potato and top with mince and cheese then return to air fryer or oven for 5 mins or until cheese is golden. Remove from air fryer/oven and top with coleslaw and sour cream. Serve.

143 Satay Chicken Bowl with Asian Greens & Rice

I've always loved satay dishes and I really love eating out of bowls (and that was before it was trendy!) so I thought, why not combine the two?! This satay chicken bowl is a healthy and easy meal for any day of the week!

 PREPTIME: 5 MIN

 COOKTIME: 30 MIN

 **SERVES:** 4 PEOPLE

INGREDIENTS

2 tbsp oil
4 chicken thighs
salt & pepper, to taste
1/2 tsp garlic salt
2 bok choy
4 tbsp smooth peanut butter
1 tbsp soy sauce
juice of 1/2 lime
1 small red chilli, finely diced
2 tbsp milk
4 tbsp water
1 cup dry white rice
2 tbsp crushed peanuts

NOTES
To make this recipe gluten-free, simply use gluten-free soy sauce

METHOD

1. Heat half the oil in a large frying pan and add chicken. Season to taste with salt, pepper and garlic salt and cook until golden. Turn over and season other side of the chicken and continue to cook until golden on both sides and cooked through.

2. Meanwhile, cut the bok choy in half lengthwise and place cut side down in the frying pan. Season with salt and cook on both sides until golden and tender. Adding a tbsp of water helps it to almost steam whilst cooking. Remove both the chicken and bok choy from pan.

3. For the satay sauce, add remaining oil to a small saucepan on medium heat. Add peanut butter, soy sauce, lime juice, chilli and milk and stir to combine. Add the water spoon by spoon, stirring to incorporate after each until the sauce is at desired consistency. Set aside.

4. Bring a pot of water to the boil and season generously with salt. Add rice and cook according to packet instructions.

5. Divide rice, bok choy and chicken between two bowls. Spoon satay sauce over each piece of chicken and sprinkle over crushed peanuts. Serve and enjoy!

144

Quick & easy Satay Chicken in a bowl!

145 Prawn, Mango & Avocado Salad

This prawn, mango and avocado salad just screams an Australian Summer! With a zesty lime dressing, it's the perfect quick meal for the scorching summer days and nights; especially when served with a refreshing cocktail to wash it down.

 PREPTIME: 5-10 MIN

 COOKTIME: 5 MIN

 **SERVES:** 4 PEOPLE

INGREDIENTS

1 tbsp oil
3 tbsp butter
2 garlic cloves, finely diced
1 lime, juiced
1kg cooked king prawns, peeled
2 cups mixed salad greens
2 mangoes, sliced
1 avocado, diced

FOR THE DRESSING
1 lime, juiced
1 tbsp olive oil
2 tbsp finely diced capsicum
1 tbsp finely chopped chives

METHOD

1. For the dressing, add lime juice, olive oil, capsicum and chives to a bowl and swirl to combine. Set aside.
2. Add oil and butter to a large frying pan on high heat. Once butter has melted, add garlic and lime juice. Add the prawns and toss, making sure they are all evenly covered in butter. Remove from pan and set aside.
3. Add salad greens, mango, avocado and prawns to a large bowl and pour over dressing. Toss thoroughly and serve.

147 Slow Cooked Beef Stroganoff

Beef Stroganoff is one of those hearty comfort foods that just seems to soothe the soul. And it's so much better cooked in a slow cooker! It's easy, it's creamy and full of flavour and the best part is you can put it on before you go to work and come home to a delicious dinner!

PREPTIME: 5 MIN

COOKTIME: 6 HOURS 30 MIN

SERVES: 4 PEOPLE

EF NF

INGREDIENTS

500g chuck steak, diced into 1.5" pieces
2 onions, sliced
2 cloves garlic, diced
500ml beef stock
1 tsp wholegrain mustard
1 1/2 tsp paprika
2 tbsp worcestershire sauce
salt & pepper, to taste
2 tbsp cornflour
1 tbsp water
5 mushrooms, sliced
150ml sour cream

NOTES

If your slow cooker doesn't have a 'sauté' setting that allows it to boil, then simply transfer to a large saucepan!

METHOD

1. Add steak, onions, garlic, stock, mustard, paprika and worcestershire sauce to a slow cooker and season to taste with salt and pepper.
2. In a small bowl, whisk together cornflour and water to form a paste and add to slow cooker. Stir to combine.
3. Cover and cook on low heat for 6 hours. Remove lid and bring to a boil, uncovered. Add mushrooms and allow to boil until most of the liquid has reduced.
4. Add sour cream and turn slow cooker off. Stir to combine and check for seasoning. Serve with mashed potato, pasta or rice.

149 Lemon & Paprika Baked Chicken

If you're after a quick and easy dinner recipe, you can't go past this baked chicken! This recipe is made with fresh lemon juice and basic spices, so it's the ultimate last minute meal!

 PREPTIME: 5 MIN

 COOKTIME: 30 MIN

 **SERVES:** 4 PEOPLE

INGREDIENTS

4 large bone-in, skin on chicken thighs
2 tbsp lemon juice
2 tbsp oil
1 tsp paprika
1 tsp garlic powder
salt & pepper, to taste

NOTES

Try serving this chicken with Garlic & Chilli Grilled Corn Cobs (p. 87)

METHOD

1. Preheat oven to 180°C and line a baking tray with baking paper.
2. Place chicken thighs in a large bowl and add lemon juice, oil, paprika and garlic powder. Toss chicken through marinade and place on prepared tray. Season to taste with salt and pepper.
3. Bake for 30 minutes or until chicken is cooked through. Serve.

151 Beef Burrito Bowls

These beef burrito bowls are a fresh and healthy Mexican inspired dinner for any day of the week! Made with ground beef mince and served with homemade guacamole and a tomato and corn salsa for the perfect toppings.

PREPTIME: 10 MIN
COOKTIME: 20 MIN
SERVES: 4 PEOPLE

GF NF EF

METHOD

1. In a large oiled frying pan on medium heat, brown off mince, breaking up big chunks until nice and small. Add spices along with 1/3 cup of water and allow to simmer until the liquid has reduced. Season to taste with salt, if necessary.
2. Meanwhile, add avocado and juice of half a lime to a bowl and mash with a fork until desired consistency. Season to taste with salt and pepper and set aside.
3. In a separate bowl, add tomato, red onion, corn and lime juice and stir well to combine. Season to taste with salt and pepper. Set aside.
4. Divide rice and meat evenly amongst four serving bowls and top with guacamole, salsa, cheese, sour cream and hot sauce, if using.

INGREDIENTS

FOR THE BEEF
1 tbsp oil
500g beef mince
2 tsp cumin
1/2 tsp onion powder
1/2 tsp garlic salt
1/2 tsp chilli powder
1/4 tsp paprika
1/8 tsp cayenne pepper
1/3 cup water
salt, to taste

FOR THE SALSA
1 tomato, diced
1 tbsp diced red onion
1 x 130g tinned corn kernels, drain
1/2 lime, juiced
salt & pepper, to taste

FOR THE GUACAMOLE
1 avocado
1/2 lime, juiced
salt & pepper, to taste

TO SERVE
2 cups cooked white rice
2 tbsp sour cream
1/2 cup grated cheese
hot sauce (optional)

155 Braised Steak & Onions

Braised steak and onions may be considered a bit of an old fashioned dish, but you can't deny how delicious it is. It's one of those classic meals that just makes you feel good inside.

 PREPTIME: 5-10 MIN

 COOKTIME: 3 HOUR 40 MIN

 SERVES: 6 PEOPLE

INGREDIENTS

1 tbsp oil
4 blade steaks (around 800g in total)
1/4 cup plain flour
6 pearl onions, quartered
3 cloves garlic, peeled and crushed
500ml beef stock
500ml water
1 bay leaf
1 tbsp worcestershire sauce
1 tbsp butter
1 tsp tomato paste
3 thyme sprigs
salt & pepper, to taste

NOTES
You can also add in some sliced carrots for a little extra flavour!

METHOD

1. Preheat oven to 125°C. Heat oil in a large dutch oven or casserole pot.
2. Cut steaks in half and coat in flour. Brown on both sides in casserole pot or dutch oven, in batches to avoid overcrowding. Remove pot from heat.
3. Add remaining ingredients and stir thoroughly to combine. Cover with a lid and place in the oven. Cook for 2 1/2 hours.
4. Turn up the heat to 180°C and remove lid. Cook for 1 hour. Remove bay leaf and thyme and serve with mashed potatoes and bread.

CHAPTER 05
Desserts

159 Chocolate Ganache Cake

This is simply the easiest homemade chocolate cake recipe ever! If you've been searching for a fuss-free cake that doesn't skimp on flavour, then look no further! This delicious chocolate cake is rich, moist and smothered in a smooth chocolate ganache icing that just adds so much to this decadent cake!

PREPTIME: 10 MIN

COOKTIME: 45-50 MIN

SERVES: 12 SLICES

INGREDIENTS

250g butter, softened to room temperature
2 cups caster sugar
4 eggs
250ml milk
2 1/2 cups plain flour
2 tsp vanilla essence
2 tsp baking powder
4 tbsp cocoa powder
200g dark cooking chocolate
100ml cream
3/4 cup icing sugar

METHOD

1. Preheat oven to 180°C and spray a 25cm round cake tin with cooking spray and line with baking paper.
2. Add butter, sugar, eggs, milk, flour, vanilla, baking powder and cocoa powder to a bowl and beat until smooth and well combined.
3. Pour batter into prepared cake tin and bake for 45-50 mins or until a skewer comes out clean. Place on a cooling rack and allow to cool completely.
4. Meanwhile, roughly chop chocolate and place it in a large heatproof bowl over a saucepan of simmering water. Add cream and stir often until melted and well combined.
5. Remove from heat and allow to cool slightly before whisking in the icing sugar. Set aside to cool completely. If icing is too runny, place in the fridge to firm up for 5-10 mins.
6. Evenly cover the cake with a layer of icing. Store leftover cake in an airtight container for up to 5 days.

NOTES
Be sure to use good quality dark chocolate for the best results.

"FOR THE BEST RESULTS,
USE GOOD QUALITY BAKING CHOCOLATE
CHEAPER BRANDS CAN OFTEN CONTAIN
HIGH AMOUNTS OF OIL WHICH CAN
CAUSE THE CHOCOLATE TO CLUMP UP"

163 Butterscotch Sauce with Banana & Ice Cream

This homemade Butterscotch Sauce recipe is a warm, gooey and decadent treat for Winter! With only five ingredients, this easy butterscotch sauce is perfect served with creamy vanilla ice cream and banana!

 PREPTIME: 2 MIN

 COOKTIME: 8 MIN

 **SERVES:** 4 PEOPLE

METHOD

1. Combine butter, sugars and water in a saucepan over medium-high heat and cook until butter has melted and sugar has dissolved.
2. Bring to the boil, then reduce heat; simmer, uncovered, without stirring for 5 mins. Remove from heat and allow the bubbles to subside. Stir in cream and serve with ice cream and bananas.

INGREDIENTS

90g butter
1/4 cup brown sugar
3/4 cup caster sugar
1/4 cup water
2/3 cup cream
8 scoops vanilla ice cream
4 small bananas

165 Passionfruit & Lemon Tart

This is a super simple and easy tart recipe to make...the no knead pastry and the three ingredient dump-and-stir filling is a winning combination for any occasion that requires a delicious dessert!

 **PREPTIME:** 15 MIN

 COOKTIME: 25 MIN

 **SERVES:** 12 SLICES

INGREDIENTS

FOR THE PASTRY
1 1/2 cups plain flour
2 tbsp icing sugar
140g cold butter
1 egg yolk
2 tbsp cold water

FOR THE FILLING
2 x 395g tins condensed milk
1/2 cup passionfruit pulp
2/3 cup lemon juice

TO SERVE
1/4 cup passionfruit pulp
whipped cream

METHOD

1. Preheat oven to 180°C and spray a round 25cm tart flan tin with a removable base with cooking spray.
2. For the pastry, blitz flour, icing sugar and butter in a food processor until it resembles a crumbly consistency. Add egg yolk and water and blitz again until it forms a ball. Wrap in plastic wrap and refrigerate for 30 mins.
3. Remove from fridge and place between two sheets of baking paper. Using a rolling pin, roll out to a 3mm thick, 32cm round circle.
4. Roll the pastry lightly around a rolling pin so that it wraps around itself and gently unroll it over the prepared tart tin. Adjust the pastry to fit into the tin and trim off any excess with a knife.
5. Prick the bottom of the pastry a few times with a fork and cover with a sheet of baking paper. Fill with baking beads or raw rice and bake for 15 mins and remove from oven. Remove paper and beads and cook for another 10 mins or until pastry is golden brown. Set aside to cool.
6. For the filling, add all ingredients to a large bowl and stir until thoroughly combined. Pour into tart shell and refrigerate for 10-15 mins or until set.
7. To serve, top with passionfruit pulp and serve with cream.

169 Chocolate Self-Saucing Pudding

Chocolate Self-Saucing Pudding is one of those dishes that warms the soul on a cold Winter's night. When the hot, gooey, saucy pudding mixes with creamy cold ice cream...that's when you know you have comfort in a bowl!

 **PREPTIME:** 10 MIN

 **COOKTIME:** 50-60 MIN

 **SERVES:** 12 PEOPLE

METHOD

1. Preheat oven to 180°C.
2. Sift flour, salt and cocoa into a large mixing bowl. Add sugar, butter, milk and vanilla and mix into a thick batter. Pour into a baking dish and spread out with a spoon.
3. For the sauce, combine sugar, cocoa and water in a medium bowl and pour over batter.
4. Bake for 50-60 mins. Serve with ice cream and fresh raspberries.

INGREDIENTS

1 cup self-raising flour
1/4 tsp salt
2 tbsp cocoa powder
3/4 cup caster sugar
30g butter, melted
1/2 cup milk
1 tsp vanilla essence

FOR THE SAUCE
3/4 cup brown sugar
1/4 cup cocoa powder
1 3/4 cups hot water

TO SERVE
ice cream
fresh raspberries

171 Banana & Cinnamon Muffins

Homemade banana & cinnamon muffins with a crunchy oat topping. Use up those overripe bananas and make these tasty muffins for morning tea, lunchboxes or an anytime snack!

PREPTIME: 10 MIN

COOKTIME: 20 MIN

MAKES: 12 MUFFINS

INGREDIENTS

1 3/4 cup self-raising flour
1/2 tsp cinnamon
3 small overripe bananas (450g)
1 cup milk
60g butter, melted
3/4 cup brown sugar

FOR TOPPING
1/2 tsp cinnamon
1/2 cup oats
1 tbsp honey

NOTES
For nice tall muffins, make sure to fill your cases right to the top!

METHOD

1. Preheat oven to 180°C and grease a 12 hole muffin tin.
2. Combine flour and cinnamon in a large bowl. Add mashed bananas, milk, butter and sugar and stir until well combined. Divide mixture evenly between muffin tin.
3. For the crunchy oat topping, combine oats, honey and cinnamon in a small bowl and stir thoroughly to combine.
4. Divide oat mixture evenly among the muffin tin and bake for 20 mins or until skewer comes out clean.
5. Enjoy as they are or serve them warm with a drizzle of maple syrup and ice cream.

173 Pecan Pie

Pecan Pie is the kind of dessert that can be served after a nice dinner or with a cuppa for morning tea and tastes just as good both times of the day. If you've never made this classic pie, now is the perfect time to try it!

 **PREPTIME:** 10-15 MIN

 **COOKTIME:** 1 HOUR

 **MAKES:** 12 SLICES

INGREDIENTS

FOR THE PASTRY
1 1/4 cups plain flour
1/3 cup icing sugar
125g cold butter, chopped
1 egg yolk
1 tsp water

FOR THE FILLING
1 cup pecans, chopped coarsely
2 tbsp cornflour
1 cup brown sugar
60g butter, melted
2 tbsp cream
1 tsp vanilla essence
3 eggs, beaten
1/3 cup pecans, whole
2 tbsp apricot jam, warmed, sieved

METHOD

1. Add flour, icing sugar and butter to a food processor and blitz until crumbly. Add egg yolk and water and blitz until ingredients just come together. Knead dough on lightly floured surface until smooth. Cover and refrigerate for 30 mins.
2. Preheat oven to 180°C and grease a 24cm-round flan tin. Roll pastry between two sheets of baking paper until large enough to line tin. Carefully ease pastry into tin, pressing into the base and sides. Trim edges.
3. Line pastry case with baking paper and fill with baking beads or raw rice. Bake for 10 mins and remove paper and beans. Bake for a further 5 mins and allow to cool. Set aside.
4. Combine chopped nuts and cornflour in a medium bowl. Add brown sugar, butter, cream, vanilla and eggs. Stir to combine. Pour mixture into shell and top with whole pecans. Bake for 45 mins and brush with jam. Serve with ice cream.

175 Puff Pastry Apple Tart

This Puff Pastry Apple Tart is an easy dessert that's still impressive! The flaky puff pastry and sweet sliced apple combo makes for the perfect way to end the evening. Sprinkle with cinnamon and sugar, drizzle on some honey and the compliments will be sure to follow.

 PREPTIME: 10 MIN

 COOKTIME: 10-15 MIN

 **MAKES:** 6 SLICES

INGREDIENTS

165g sheet ready-made puff pasty, thawed
1 large apple, peeled, cored and sliced
2 tsp caster sugar
1/2 tsp ground cinnamon
1 egg, beaten
2 tsp honey

METHOD

1. Preheat oven to 180°C and line a large baking tray with baking paper.
2. Place pastry on prepared baking tray and, using the back of a knife, score a 3/4 inch border around the edge, making sure it doesn't cut all the way through.
3. Arrange the apple so that all the slices are touching each other tightly.
4. Evenly sprinkle sugar and cinnamon over apple and brush the edge of the pastry with egg using a pastry brush.
5. Bake for 10-15 mins or until the edge of the pastry is golden brown and the apple slices are soft and tender.
6. Remove from oven and drizzle over honey whilst still hot. Serve warm or at room temperature.

177 Plain Baked Cheesecake

Plain Baked Cheesecake is hands down my favourite kind of cheesecake. It's decadent and creamy and also pretty simple to whip up on a weekend! And if I can add one last thing, it's that you should definitely serve it with fresh strawberries!

PREPTIME: 15-20 MIN

COOKTIME: 1 HOUR 35 MIN

MAKES: 12 SLICES

INGREDIENTS

250g plain sweet biscuits
150g butter, melted
750g cream cheese, softened
2 tsp lemon zest, finely grated
1 cup caster sugar
3 eggs
1 cup sour cream
1/4 cup lemon juice

FOR THE TOPPING
1 cup sour cream
2 tbsp caster sugar
2 tsp lemon juice
1 tsp ground nutmeg

NOTES
Using a flat drinking glass helps to level out the biscuit base!

METHOD

1. Preheat oven to 180°C and line a 24cm springform pan. Set aside.
2. Using a food processor, blitz biscuits until fine. Add butter and blitz until well combined. Press into prepared pan, spreading it about 2-3 inches up the side. Using a spoon, spread out the mixture until even. Place on an oven tray and refrigerate for 30 mins.
3. Meanwhile, beat cream cheese, lemon zest and sugar in a medium bowl with an electric mixer until smooth. Beat in eggs, one at a time, then sour cream and lemon juice. Beat until thoroughly combined.
4. Pour filling into prepared tin and bake 1 1/4 hours. Remove from oven and allow to cool for 15-20 mins.
5. To make the topping, add sour cream, sugar and lemon juice to a small bowl and stir to combine.
6. Spread sour cream mixture over cooled cheesecake and sprinkle over nutmeg. Bake for a further 20 mins. Allow to cool in oven with the door ajar. Refrigerate for 3 hours or overnight. Serve with fresh berries.

181 Mini Pavlova with Whipped Cream & Fruit

Pavlova has to be one of the best summer desserts there is. Crispy on the outside, chewy on the inside and loaded with whipped cream and fresh fruit! Yes please!

 PREPTIME: 5-10 MIN

 COOKTIME: 2 HOURS

 **MAKES:** 8 PAVLOVAS

INGREDIENTS

4 large egg whites, at room temperature
pinch of salt
3/4 cup caster sugar
2 tsp cornflour
1 tsp vanilla essence
1/2 cup thickened cream
2 tbsp icing sugar
fresh strawberries
fresh blueberries
fresh kiwifruit

METHOD

1. Preheat oven to 110°C. Prepare a baking tray with baking paper and set aside. Using an electric beater, beat the egg whites and salt until soft peaks form. Gradually add the sugar, whisking well between each addition, until thick and glossy and all the sugar has dissolved. Carefully fold in the cornflour and vanilla essence.
2. Spoon the meringue evenly onto baking tray into 8 even circles. Spread the meringue out over each circle.
3. Cook for 1 hour or until the meringues are crisp. Turn the oven off and use a wooden spoon to keep the door ajar. Set aside in the oven for around an hour or until cooled completely.
4. Meanwhile, add cream and icing sugar to a small bowl and beat until thoroughly whipped.
5. To serve, add a dollop of cream to each pavlova and top with cut up fresh fruit.

A classic Aussie favourite!

183 Caramel Mud Cake

Something that's called 'caramel mud cake' sounds rich and sweet, but I assure you that this cake is the perfect level of decadence! You can serve this cake cold or warm with either whipped cream or ice cream for the perfect treat.

 PREPTIME: 5-10 MIN

 COOKTIME: 45-50 MIN

 **MAKES:** 12 SLICES

INGREDIENTS

200g butter, cubed
200g white chocolate, chopped
1 cup brown sugar
3/4 cup hot water
1 tbsp golden syrup
1 tsp vanilla essence
2 eggs
1 cup plain flour
1 cup self-raising flour
icing sugar, to dust

METHOD

1. Preheat oven to 180°C and line a 22cm round cake tin with baking paper. Set aside.
2. Place butter, chocolate, sugar, water, syrup and vanilla in a large saucepan on medium heat and stir with a metal spoon until chocolate has melted and mixture is smooth. Set aside for 20 mins to cool.
3. Add eggs, one at a time, to the caramel mixture and whisk well to combine. Add flour and stir until mixture is thoroughly combined.
4. Pour into prepared cake tin and bake for 45-50 mins or until a metal skewer comes out clean.
5. Allow cake to cool for 15-20 mins before dusting with icing sugar. Serve with whipped cream or ice cream.

Strawberries & Chocolate Ganache

Strawberries with chocolate ganache has to be the ultimate sweet pairing! And this recipe couldn't be easier to make, with only three ingredients! It's pure indulgence!

 **PREPTIME:** 2 MIN

 **COOKTIME:** 15-20 MIN

 **SERVES:** 6-8 PEOPLE

    GF V NF EF

INGREDIENTS

300g dark baking chocolate
150ml heavy cream
1/4 cup icing sugar
250g strawberries

METHOD

1. Roughly chop chocolate and place in a large heatproof bowl over a saucepan of simmering water. Add cream.
2. Stir the cream and chocolate often until melted and well combined. Remove from heat and allow to cool slightly before whisking in icing sugar.
3. Let cool for 10-15 mins in the fridge and pour into a serving bowl. Serve with strawberries.

NOTES
You can also serve this ganache with chopped up banana and marshmallows or you can use it as icing for chocolate cake.

191 Orange & Poppyseed Cake

This cake is the perfect thing for a quick afternoon tea! It's light and fluffy and has a refreshing citrus taste that makes it irresistible -especially served with a nice cup of tea!

 **PREPTIME:** 5-10 MIN

 **COOKTIME:** 45-50 MIN

 **MAKES:** 12 SLICES

INGREDIENTS
60g butter, room temperature
1/3 cup caster sugar
1 tsp vanilla essence
1 egg
1/4 cups fresh orange juice
1 tbsp orange zest, plus extra to garnish
1 1/4 cup self-raising flour
1/2 cup milk
1/2 tsp poppy seeds

FOR THE ICING
1 cup icing sugar, sifted
1 tbsp milk
1 tbsp fresh orange juice

METHOD

1. Preheat oven to 180°C and line a ring cake pan with baking paper. Spray the edges with cooking spray and set aside.
2. Beat together butter and sugar with an electric mixer until pale and creamy. Add vanilla, egg, orange juice and zest and beat to combine.
3. Sift flour and add to mixture alternately with milk. Add poppyseeds and continue to beat until thoroughly combined.
4. Pour batter into prepared cake tin and bake for 45-50 mins or until a metal skewer comes out clean. Allow to cool completely before turning out onto a cooling rack.
5. For the icing, combine icing sugar, milk and orange juice in a bowl. Drizzle over cooled cake and allow to set before serving. Decorate with orange zest if desired.

193 Mixed Berry Cheesecake Slice

This Mixed Berry Cheesecake Slice is creamy bite sized goodness! And definitely the perfect recipe for entertaining. It is sure to be a hit at any morning tea!

 **PREPTIME:** 20 MIN

 **COOKTIME:** 30 MIN

 **MAKES:** 20 SLICES

INGREDIENTS

1 x 395g tin condensed milk
2 eggs
500g cream cheese
2 tbsp lemon juice
1 tsp vanilla essence
1 cup mixed frozen berries
150g butter, melted
250g plain sweet biscuits
fresh berries, to serve
whipped cream, to serve (optional)

METHOD

1. Preheat oven to 150°C and line a 20cm x 30cm slice tin with baking paper, allowing the sides to overhang.
2. Crush biscuits in a food processor until fine. Add the butter and stir until thoroughly combined. Spoon mixture into the slice tin and flatten out, making sure the base is level and even. Place in the fridge to cool for 30 mins.
3. Meanwhile, beat cream cheese with an electric beater until smooth. Add condensed milk, lemon juice and vanilla and beat again until smooth. Add eggs and beat until well combined.
4. Add berries to cream cheese mixture and gently stir through with a spatula or spoon. Pour mixture onto biscuit base and smooth out with spatula.
5. Bake for 30 mins or until just set and turn the oven off. Cool in the oven, with the door slightly ajar for 1 hour. Place in the fridge for 2 hours, or overnight to chill. Cut into squares and serve with whipped cream.

195 Chocolate Cream Pie

Chocolate Cream Pie. What more could I say? This is the kind of dessert you bring out when you're craving something decadent. It's creamy, smooth and oh so delicious!

PREPTIME: 20-25 MIN

COOKTIME: 35 MIN

MAKES: 12 SLICES

INGREDIENTS

FOR THE PASTRY
1 1/2 cups plain flour
2 tbsp icing sugar
140g cold butter, chopped
1 egg yolk
2 tbsp cold water

FOR THE FILLING
2/3 cup caster sugar
pinch of salt
1 1/2 cups milk
2 tbsp cornflour
3 egg yolks
175g dark cooking chocolate, chopped
40g butter, chopped
1 tsp vanilla essence

FOR THE TOPPING
300ml thickened cream
1/4 cup icing sugar
dark chocolate, to garnish

METHOD

1. For the pastry, preheat oven to 220°C and spray a 24cm pie tin with cooking spray. Set aside.
2. Add flour, icing sugar and butter to a food processor and blitz until crumbly. Add egg yolk and water and blitz until the dough forms a ball. Wrap in plastic wrap and refrigerate for 30 mins.
3. On a lightly floured surface, roll out the dough with a rolling pin into an 11-inch circle. Fold the dough over the rolling pin then gently unroll it over the pie tin. Smooth the dough into the pan, making sure to press down into the shape of the tin. Line with baking paper and fill with baking beads or raw rice.
4. Bake for 15 mins and carefully remove baking beans. Bake for a further 10 mins and remove from oven. Allow to cool for at least 10 mins.
5. For the filling, add sugar, salt and milk to a medium saucepan on medium heat and whisk to combine. Bring to a gentle simmer, whisking frequently.
6. Meanwhile, combine cornflour and egg yolks in a small bowl and whisk until smooth and well combined. Set aside.
7. Once the milk mixture is simmering, add a few spoonfuls of the liquid to the egg yolks, whisking after each spoonful to temper the eggs. Add a few more spoonfuls to the eggs then slowly whisk the egg mixture into the saucepan. Whisk constantly until the mixture begins to thicken and bring it to a gentle boil.
8. Remove saucepan from the heat and stir through chocolate, butter and vanilla until completely smooth. Pour the filling into cooled pie crust and refrigerate for 3 hours or overnight.
9. Add cream and icing sugar to a mixing bowl and beat on high speed until the cream forms soft peaks. Spread whipped cream over pie. Using a microplane or lemon zester, grate chocolate over whipped cream and serve.

197 Lemon & Raspberry Loaf Cake

This lemon and raspberry loaf cake is an easy sweet treat that's perfect for morning tea! This buttery loaf cake recipe is made with fresh lemon juice and raspberries then topped off with a delicious glaze icing! It's sure to be a family favourite!

PREPTIME: 10 MIN

COOKTIME: 20-25 MIN

MAKES: 12 SLICES

INGREDIENTS
60g butter
1/3 cup caster sugar
1 egg
1 tsp vanilla essence
1/2 lemon, juiced
1 1/4 cups self-raising flour
1/2 cup milk
1/2 cup raspberries, plus extra for serving
1 cup icing sugar
1 tsp vanilla essence
2-3 tbsp milk

METHOD
1. Preheat oven to 180°C and prepare a 9×5 inch loaf tin with baking paper.
2. Beat butter and sugar until creamy. Add egg, vanilla and lemon juice and beat until well combined.
3. Add flour and milk alternately, scraping down the sides to make sure everything is combined. Gently stir through raspberries.
4. Pour cake batter into prepared loaf tin and bake for 20-25 mins or until a metal skewer comes out clean. Transfer to a cooling rack.
5. Once the cake has cooled, combine icing sugar and vanilla, then add the milk 1 tbsp at a time, adding more or less as needed. The icing should be thick and not too runny. Pour over cake and allow to set before serving. Garnish with raspberries if desired.

INDEX

A

Air Fryer; Crispy Chicken Legs....................127
Apple, Rocket & Pine Nut Salad.......................97
Apple; Puff Pastry Tart....................175
Asian Beef & Noodle Soup..............125
Avocado; Prawn & Mango Salad..................145

B

Bacon & Egg Toast Cups.................................25
Banana & Cinnamon Muffins.......................171
Basic Pancakes....................................11
Beef & Horseradish Sliders........................113
Beef Burrito Bowls................................151
Beef; Asian Noodle Soup......................125
Beef; Slow Cooked Stroganoff........................147
Beet; Slow Cooker Ragu......................107
Beetroot & Pistachio Dip.................................57
Beetroot, Red Onion & Feta Tarte Tatin..............53
Berry; Mixed Cheesecake Slice....................193
Braised Steak & Onions.................................155
Breakfast Board..13
Brekky Wraps..21
Broccoli; Cheese Stuffed Chicken.................121
Bruschetta; Tomato..................................55
Butter Chicken......................................137
Butterscotch Sauce with Banana..................163

C

Cake; Caramel Mud................................183
Cake; Chocolate Ganache............................159
Cake; Lemon & Raspberry Loaf.....................197
Cake; Orange & Poppyseed....................191
Capsicum; Roasted Dip...........................61
Caramel Mud Cake................................183
Cheats Tortilla Chips..71
Cheese & Broccoli Stuffed Chicken..............121
Cheesecake; Mixed Berry........................193
Cheesecake; Plain Baked......................177
Cheesy Bacon Potatoes...........................89
Cheesy Spinach Omelette........................35
Chicken & Vegetable Soup......................115
Chicken Maryland Traybake.....................109
Chicken; Butter....................................137
Chicken; Cheese & Broccoli Stuffed............121
Chicken; Crispy Air Fryer Legs.................127
Chicken; Greek Skewers........................133
Chicken; Lemon & Paprika Baked..............149
Chicken; Mini Curry Pot Pies.....................103
Chicke; Satay Bowl with Asian Greens.........143
Chicken; Sticky Honey-Soy Wings................65
Chilli Con Carne....................................101
Chips; Cheats Tortilla..............................71
Chips; Homemade with Tuna Patties..........105
Chips; Lime & Black Pepper Potato.............73
Chocolate Cream Pie............................195
Chocolate Ganache Cake......................159
Chocolate Self-Saucing Pudding..............169
Chocolate; Strawberries & Ganache...........187
Classic Cob Loaf....................................51
Corn Cobs; Garlic Buttered......................87
Creamy French Baked Eggs......................37
Crispy Air Fryer Chicken Legs..................127

D

Dip; Beetroot & Pistachio.........................57
Dip; Mediterranean Layer White Bean..........67
Dip; Roasted Capsicum Bean....................61
Dip; Spinach & Feta...............................59

E

Easy Greek Salad................................81
Easy Shakshuka..................................27
Eggs; Bacon Toast Cups........................25
Eggs; Creamy French Baked.....................37

F

Fettuccine Carbonara................................135
French Toast with Bacon & Maple Syrup......31
Fresh Tomato Salsa (Pico de Gallo)..............69

G

Garlic Buttered Grilled Corn Cobs................87
Greek Chicken Skewers.............................133

H

Homemade Battered Onion Rings.................85

L

Lamb; Roast Leg with Mint Sauce..............117
Leek; & Potato Soup.............................45
Leeks; Sautéed with Garlic Chilli Oil............83
Lemon & Paprika Baked Chicken..............149
Lemon & Raspberry Loaf Cake................197
Lemon; Passionfruit Tart.......................165
Lime & Black Pepper Potato Chips.............73

INDEX

M

Mediterranean Layer White Bean Dip..........67
Mini Chicken Curry Pot Pies........................103
Mini Pavlova with Whipped Cream............181
Mint Sauce; with Roast Leg of Lamb..........117
Mixed Berry Cheesecake Slice....................193
Mud Cake; Caramel.................................183
Muffins; Banana & Cinnamon....................171
Mushroom Sauce; with Ribeye Steak..........131

N

Nachos; Pico de Gallo.................................49

O

Omelette; Cheesy Spinach..........................35
Onion Rings; Homemade Battered..............85
Orange & Poppyseed Cake.......................191

P

Pancakes; Basic..11
Passionfruit & Lemon Tart.......................165
Pavlova; Mini with Whipped Cream............181
Pecan Pie...173
Pico de Gallo Nachos................................49
Pie; Chocolate Cream..............................195
Pie; Pecan..173
Pie; Mini Chicken Curry...........................103
Pistachio; Beetroot Dip..............................57
Plain Baked Cheesecake.........................177
Potato & Leek Soup..................................45
Potato; Lime & Black Pepper Chips............73
Potato; Cheesy Bacon...............................89
Potato; Savoury Mince & Coleslaw...........141
Potato; Sour Cream & Chives....................93
Potato; Spinach & Pumpkin.......................91
Prawn, Mango & Avocado Salad..............145
Puff Pastry Apple Tart.............................175

Q

Quick & Easy Spaghetti Marinara................47

R

Raspberry; Lemon Loaf Cake..................197
Ribeye Steak with Mushroom Sauce........131
Roast Leg of Lamb with Mint Sauce.........117
Roasted Capsicum Bean Dip.....................61

S

Salad; Apple, Rocket & Pine Nut..............97
Salad; Easy Greek...................................81
Salad; Prawn, Mango & Avocado............145
Salad; Warm Zucchini, Feta & Pine Nut....77
Salsa; Fresh Tomato................................69
Satay Chicken Bowl with Asian Greens...143
Sausage & Potato Breakfast Hash............33
Sautéed Leeks with Garlic & Chilli Oil......83
Savoury Mince & Coleslaw Potatoes......141
Savoury Mince & Egg..............................19
Shakshuka; Easy....................................27
Skewers; Greek Chicken.......................133
Slow Cooked Beef Stroganoff................147
Slow Cooker Beef Ragu.........................107
Smashed Avo with Feta..........................23
Soup; Asian Beef & Noodle...................125
Soup; Chicken & Vegetable....................115
Soup; Potato & Leek..............................45
Sour Cream & Chives Potatoes...............93
Spaghetti Marinara; Quick & Easy..........47
Spinach & Feta Dip................................59
Spinach & Pumpkin Potatoes.................91
Spinach; Cheesy Omelette.....................35
Steak; Braised Onions.........................155
Steak; Ribeye with Mushroom Sauce.....131
Sticky Honey-Soy Chicken Wings..........65
Strawberries & Chocolate Ganache.........187
Stuffed Breakfast Tomatoes....................15

T

Tart; Passionfruit & Lemon...................165
Tart; Puff Pastry Apple.........................175
Tomato Bruschetta................................55
Tomato; Fresh Salsa..............................69
Tomatoes; Stuffed Breakfast.................15
Tortilla Chips...71
Tuna Patties with Homemade Chips......105

W

Warm Zucchini, Feta & Pine Nut Salad......77

Z

Zucchini; Warm Feta & Pine Nut Salad......77

WANT MORE?

For more recipes, articles & foodie finds, join the conversation on our social media networks! Follow @kjsfoodjournal today!

kjsfoodjournal.com

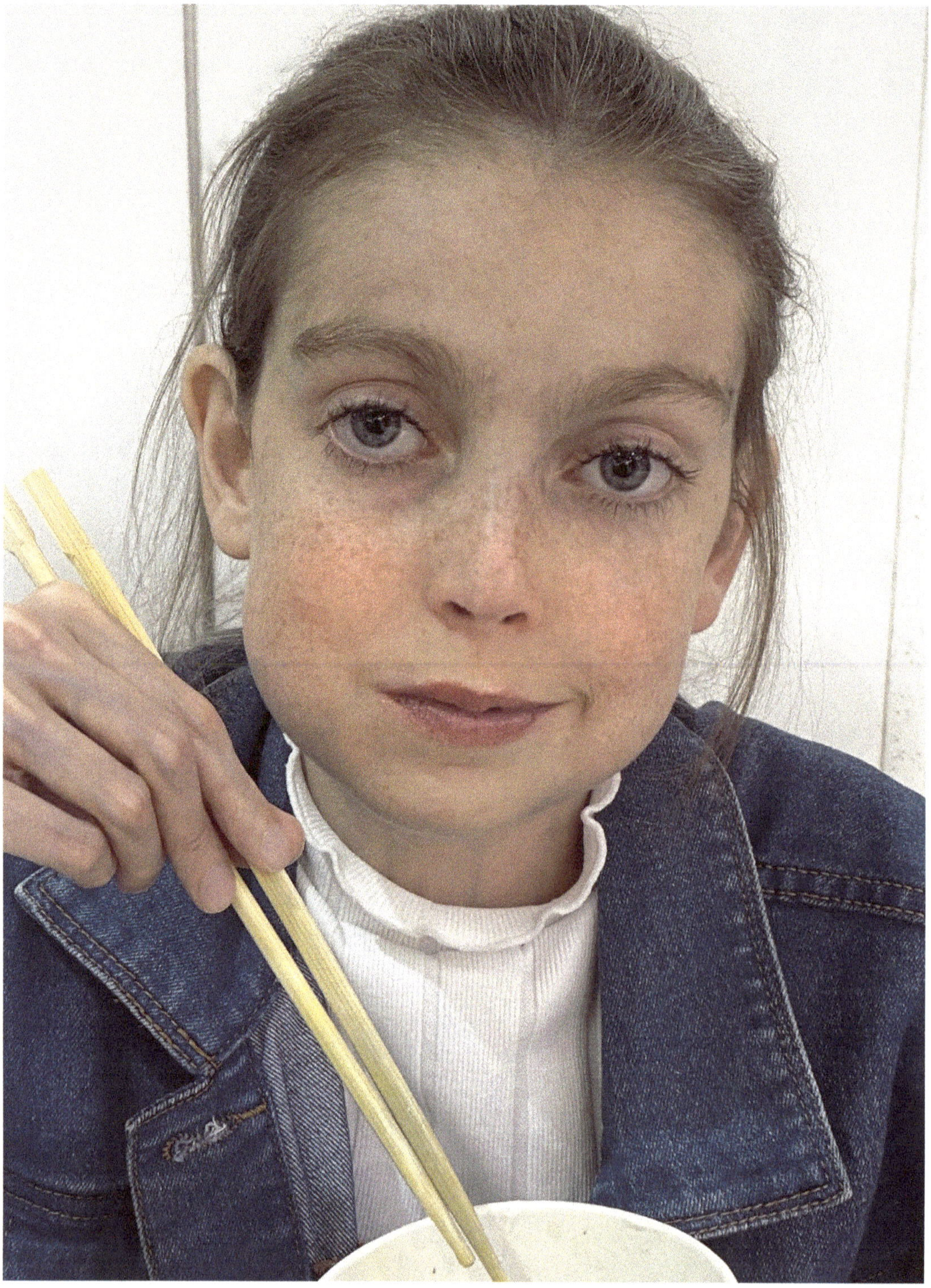

© Kj's Food Journal 2024 | All rights reserved
kjsfoodjournal.com |
kjsfoodjournal@outlook.com
Photography : Keeley Spencer